When
I Was Little
I Used to Be
Colored

THE STORY
OF LIFE
IN A REAL
VILLAGE

Carl A. Benson Sr.

authorHOUSE®

AuthorHouse™
1663 Liberty Drive
Bloomington, IN 47403
www.authorhouse.com
Phone: 1-800-839-8640

Published by AuthorHouse   10/27/2012

ISBN: 978-1-4772-8541-1 (sc)
ISBN: 978-1-4772-8751-4 (hc)
ISBN: 978-1-4772-8542-8 (e)

Library of Congress Control Number: 2012920358

Dedicated to my brother Billy Jones

Who taught me everything I needed to know to become a man

INTRODUCTION

WHAT A CURIOUS BOOK TITLE, "When I Was Little I Used to Be Colored." When my wife heard it the first thing she asked was "Well, what are we now?" I answered we're African Americans, Democrats, Republicans, Presbyterians, Methodists, Liberals, Conservatives, Suburbanites, Los Angelinos, Middle Class, Rich, Famous, Baptists, Executives, Professionals, Muslims, Gang Bangers. These labels which we so proudly clutch to our breasts define us rather than us defining them.

This title was not selected because of a play on words. No. It represents a point in time when we were a different people. A time when we were truly a neighborhood, family, as Hillary says, a village. We cared for each other, talked to each other, not suing each other; we lived together, played together, cried together. We fed each other, clothed each other, we prayed together and loved each other. Why? Because "we" were all we had. We had what I like to call Peoplehood. We stood for something and we knew what it was. This is going to come as a shock to those who know me and what I fought for in the sixties and seventies, but we lost our village mentality when we integrated. Those of us with garages have opted out of village life by being able to drive into a garage and push a button and have the garage door shut the rest of the world out. I am not advocating going back to a segregated society but I am advocating re-awakening that community spirit, village spirit, we used to have *when we were colored.*

When you read this book I hope it stirs up memories that make you remember what the village life was like, and make you long to get it back. Maybe it will make you want to gather the family together and talk about your village life, and laugh until your sides ache with joy. The names have been changed for obvious reasons but the names do not alter the story or the characters.

Some of us are getting older and may not see the village return, but we remember what it was like and can talk to the younger folks about its meaning. We must regain it or be so overwhelmed with selfless individualism that we can never come together again in the village. Let us become story tellers to our families and friends. Pull those old pictures out of the basement or attic and go through them and talk about your childhood, your mother's childhood, pass the stories along. We mustn't lose our glorious heritage back when we were colored. Enjoy

Chapter 1   In The Beginning

WHEN I WAS LITTLE I USED TO BE COLORED. I know that because when I talk about my childhood with other Black people, guess what, it's similar to their childhood. So similar you'd think we were all related. But we could have been raised in Cleveland or Los Angeles and the experiences are nearly the same. I guess poor people have poor ways where ever they live. And why not, it was our only exposure at the time. *When we were colored.*

I knew we were colored because the old folks used to refer to ourselves as "colored". My grandmother would talk about "the colored man over there or the colored lady with the blue hat, or colored people ought to do this or that". Once in a while she would talk about the "colored only" signs in the south. But my grandmother was not fazed or intimidated by any of that stuff. She would drag us "chilren" on a streetcar or bus without paying a fare and tell us to "gwon sit down". Even after the protests of the drivers Mama would just ignore them and pay one fare for herself and sit down next to us.

As a child, being colored didn't feel bad or different, it was what we were. And as long as we could have a scoop of orange sherbet in a cup once in a while, or a piece of candy occasionally, or a piece of sweet potato pie, being colored wasn't bad.

Cleveland was always grey. The sky never looked blue to me even when it was. I guess it was because in the part of town where we lived there were factories and steel mills near by and they kept the sky filled with smoke or other pollutants. When I went to visit my aunt on E. 31st street I could see the open flames from the coke mills burning 24 hours it seems.

Cleveland was like looking at an old black and white news reel every day. Our house was grey, all the cars were grey, the trees in our neighborhood were grey, and the children were grey. At least, that's the way it looked to me when I was a little boy. But as I grew older and ventured out to other neighborhoods, or to the once a year pilgrimage to the Cleveland Zoo, or Geauga Lake to the Weatherhead Annual Picnic for its workers, I would see that other parts of Cleveland were not grey like our neighborhood. But our neighborhood was a special place; a place where we could run around free from terror, or drugs, gangs or other outside influences that could cause a kid to develop bad habits.

Back in the forties and fifties we had a neighborhood. Just like Richard Pryor's drunk character said, it was a "neighborhood not a residential district." The cobblestone streets were laid out in numerical order. Ours happened to be E. 65th Street. Each street was separated by an alley, which served not only as a place to park your car, but for recreational purposes. We often played in the alley, and, the numbers people used it to play their illegal gambling games. Every now and then the police would raid a game and people would scatter like roaches in a cabinet when you turned a light on.

The houses were primarily wooden siding with front porches and back porches. Occasionally you would see a brick house, usually a two family house with a family upstairs and one downstairs. On our block there was a vacant lot halfway down the block which lent itself to a friendly softball game often.

To our detriment as kids, all of the neighbors knew all of the kids, and our parents. And often, a neighbor's call would precede your arrival at home where a parent would be waiting with a belt to "whup" you for something the neighbor had reported. Parents were grateful for the neighborhood lookouts and there was never a hint of litigation or threat of a fist fight for a neighbor dragging you home to report on your behavior. It often acted as a deterrent to us because we knew which neighbors would tell on us and we avoided doing anything questionable in those areas. You try this today and not only would you get sued, you will probably have to fight your way back home.

On the whole, the properties were pretty well maintained, even though most of them were not owned by the occupants. Some yards were fenced in and sported grass and shrubbery. Some yards had no grass and were usually where kids lived or played regularly. Our yard had no grass for as long as I can remember and was the gathering place for most of the neighborhood kids. Our yard was the ideal place to play. We had a big tree in the front yard, no grass so we could shoot marbles or play "chubby" there (Root a Peg or Mumbly Peg to some). There was a telephone pole on the side of the driveway which was perfect for Hide the Paddle. I can still hear the song we sang while leaning against the pole waiting for everyone to hide. It went "Last night and the night before, twenty-four robbers at my door. I got up to let them in, hit 'em in the head with a rolling pin. Ready or not here I come". Then, the count to ten. We would scatter and by the time the caller got to ten, there were no children in sight. There were so many hiding places in our two or three house area of play; you could never find all of the players. They were constantly running back to the pole before the caller could hit them with a paddle, or stick.

Chapter 2

PICTURE: THIS IS EAST 65TH STREET in Cleveland, Ohio where I was raised. This is our "village". The light post on the right is where we played Hide and Go Seek, Hide the Paddle, and It. Right in the middle of the street next to the post is where I had a fight with a kid from the next block over, and where he stuck me in the eye with a broken broom handle. We played stick ball, Set-Back and held track meets here. We also raised a PhD in Chemistry, several school teachers, an NCAA track hurdles champion, A Post Master of the Cleveland Branch of the U.S. Post Office, and me of course. If you look to the right sidewalk you can hear Mr. Bradley coming home on Saturday night, a little tipsy, singing, "It's a long way to Tipperary".

Our neighborhood was very colorful; we had very interesting families and characters up and down the block. All the way at the end of the street at the opposite direction as the picture shows was my best friend Nate. He lived by the gully at the end of the block that went down to the railroads tracks. The gully was an urban legend in itself having had the reputation that a killer lurked there. A story went around that a human head had been found there by children taking the shortcut through there on the way to school. We never knew who those children were incidentally but that never stopped us boys from using the shortcut while secretly looking for heads on the path down the gully.

The gully had a more useful purpose also. The coal trains that passed through there often dropped lumps of coal along the tracks and we would go down there and gather a bushel basket full to burn in our pot belly stoves in the winter. The trains would also drop pieces of iron or steel from the mills and we gathered them up for sale to the junk man.

Further up from the gully was a family I'll call the Harkins. It is said that Aaron Neville has the world's most beautiful voice, but the world never heard Eugene Harkins sing unfortunately. Eugene would lead all of the songs while we do wopped on the corner of 65th and Woodland. Still to this day I have never heard a more beautiful version of The Irish Lullaby sung by any professional, anywhere. Not even the Irish.

One of the most unique characteristics of our neighborhood was the Junk Yard on the west side of the street. This yard had a horse barn and the horse was used to pull the old wooden wagon full of junk up and down the street. I can still hear the junk man's cry of "Ehhh pa dehhp, ehhh pa dehhp". Upon hearing that call we would run out to the street to pet the huge horse that stood patiently as junk was loaded on the wagon. After a few years the horse and the old white man disappeared from the street and that call was never heard again until Oscar Brown, Jr. sang about Rags and Old Iron in his hit song years later.

In the middle of the block was a family with a boy and a girl. I think the boy's name was Earl, and the girl's name was Russia. What I do remember about the girl is that she was as black as night and every bit as beautiful. Her skin was flawless and the girl had back. Unfortunately she was easy and all of the boys on the block were pursuing her sweet caresses. I was one of them.

Three doors from the beauty lived the Simons family. There were four boys, Donnie, Billy, Arnet and Marvin, and one girl, Tina. Billy was my boy and we went everywhere together. Billy was light-skinned and good looking and was the best hand dancer I'd ever seen. We would go to the Blue Jean Dance at the roller rink every Saturday night and turn it out. You see, I was the second best dancer I ever saw. The girls would literally line up to dance with Billy and me and we took advantage of the attention it brought us. Billy could do a twirl which today would equate to a quadruple Sow Kow in figure skating, and catch the hand of the girl before she could turn one time. We had reputations and followings on both the east and west sides of Cleveland. I went to a near neighborhood block party once and entered the dance contest and won hands down, with a girlfriend from high school.

Billy Simons was my next door neighbor and our houses were so close together we used to open our side windows and pass funny books or other things to each other. It was in Billy's back yard that I learned how to wring a chicken's neck and kill a turtle to make turtle soup. Billy's Grandfather and Grandmother were the class of the neighborhood and brought experiences most of us never knew before. Mr. Simons took us fishing at Put In Bay on Lake Erie near Sandusky, Ohio and let us ride his horse named Copek which was stabled near Akron. The Simons' were like a Headstart Program in the fifties for our neighborhood. They grew their own vegetables and had the prettiest yards on the block.

Chapter 3

MY HOUSE WAS A TWO FAMILY wood frame house with the landlady Mrs. Hawkins living upstairs with her son Howard. Howard was a nice guy and would let me pal around with him some even though he was a few years older than I. Once while looking for Howard up in his home, I had the scariest experience of my life. I still remember it today, vividly. I went upstairs to see Howard and the door was open and the lights were off in the house. I called and called and there was no answer. As I walked from the kitchen to the dining room I ran into a man's figure dressed in black. My mind immediately perceived the image of the Devil, black clothes, red silk lined cape, horny head. It scared me so badly I don't think I ever went upstairs again. To me then and to me now, it was real. It's making my hair stand up as I'm writing this.

Our house downstairs was a two bedroom with one bathroom. The bathroom was off the kitchen in the back of the house, and the formal dining room was off to the right corner of the kitchen. A bedroom was to the back of the dining room and that is where my Aunt Jeanette and Uncle William, whom we all called Daddy, slept. I had been raised by my aunt and uncle who were the only real parents I and my sister Barbara knew. Jen had four children of her own, Billy, Jackie, Jerry and Andy. We were all brothers and sister, one family, even today. My mother was living in Cincinnati with my Step-father Bishop O.W. Nickerson.

The living room was off the dining room in the front of the house and it had a magnificent fireplace which never worked and a mantel which held pictures of relatives. It also held a picture of a ship at sea. The sea was angry and the ship looked like was in trouble. When I asked Jen what the picture represented, she said, the Wreck of Hesperus. I didn't understand what that meant until later in life when I looked it up in an encyclopedia and found it was a famous picture from a famous piece of literature.

In the window of the living room hung a cardboard placard with three black stars on a white background. As a child I didn't understand what this meant until my grandmother explained it to me. Each star represented a family member, in this case uncles, who were serving in the military during World War II. Our three stars represented my three uncles James and Charles in the Army, and Fred in the Navy. When Charles came home he would tell us stories about his time in Italy as a member of the Transportation Division, truck drivers. Charles talked about the segregated Army and how colored soldiers were only allowed to cook or drive trucks. As a truck driver they were camped in Italy one night when gunfire rang out in the camp from a sniper. Not having been in combat the drivers scrambled like cats all over the camp looking for a place to hide. My uncle Charles being one of the scramblers considered himself lucky when he found a mound to hide in. The mound turned out to be a mound of human waste and he dove in head first. He said he didn't stop to analyze the make up of the mound of stuff at least until after the sniper fire ceased.

You can imagine what he smelled like when he extracted himself from the pile of crap but he was still alive. This must have been the time when someone said "War is hell."

When my uncles returned from the service in 1945 they still found America the same as when they left, segregated and racist. They did not return heroes with special treatment from the community or the nation; they were still unemployed and still "colored" in the eyes of white America.

It wasn't until 1948 that President Harry S. Truman, needing the colored vote integrated the Army in an effort to garnish the support of colored voters. It worked for him, he won the election. Ironically, this was not the first time in history that the American Army was integrated. Without giving you an American history lesson here I can tell you that unknowingly a colored man named Crispus Attucks became the first person to die in the Revolutionary War in 1775 outside a Boston bar, and the war that ensued would include thousands of colored participants.

The 54th Massachusetts Infantry would fight valiantly and prove the capabilities of colored soldiers to participant further in the war. A colored woman, Deborah Gannett, disguised as a man would become a decorated soldier in that war and George Washington lifted the ban on the use of colored soldiers in 1776 which resulted in over 5,000 colored soldiers fighting beside white soldiers helping to win the war that created our United States of America.

In every war history record Colored, Negro, Black, or African Americans fought beside white soldiers and helped to keep America free. Even today our soldiers are prominent in the War against Terrorism, fighting, and dying to maintain our freedoms. And you know, the same thing happens today as it did when my uncle Charles returned from the World War II in 1945, we are still discriminated against and taken for granted by a major part of society.

No matter how many persons of color die or leave their blood on foreign soil, nothing changes when we get back home to America. I guess it will be the "next war" that gives us enough credits to be equal, real Americans. If we still put stars in the window for our sons, brothers and sisters who serve in wars, we couldn't see out of the window today. It would be covered with stars.

CHAPTER 4

AS CHILDREN WE HUDDLED AROUND the floor model radio in the living room to listen to such shows as Happy Hank singing "*Merci do and doci do a little lambsy lidy, afiddly diddly do wouldn't you?*", Red Rider and Little Beaver, Bobby Benson and the B-Bar-B Riders, the Inner Sanctum, the Sheriff, My Friend Irma, Friday Night Fights, the Thin Man, Fibber McGhee and Molly, Amos and Andy, and The Shadow (who knows what lurks in the hearts of men, the Shadow "do".).

The second bedroom was to the left of the living room and had a full bed by the front window and bunk beds on the wall. My Grandmother slept in the bed by the window and my sister slept in the top bunk. When I was little I slept with my Grandmother and it was a constant battle every night not to get crushed by big Momma when she turned over at night. The bottom bunk was occupied at different times by two of the other kids. Later on we got a Hide Away Bed for the dining room after Billy, the oldest and the athlete in the family moved out and got married.

Life was fairly normal, or at least felt normal when I was colored, until the rats chewed their way into the interior of the house. We would see them in the kitchen behind the water heater or in the bathroom. Every time we would patch up the holes they entered from they made new ones. It got so bad that before the two younger boys went to bed I made sure that they did not have food particles around their mouths so the rats would not nibble on them.

It was not unusual that I would wake up in the middle of the night and chase the rats away from the other kid's beds. That may have contributed to my insomnia today because I couldn't sleep thinking about the rats. I used to sit up all night watching television until it signed off. It became a routine thing and I assumed that every body lived like that. I never talked about it with friends at school; it was how poor people lived. *When I was colored.*

During my teenage years things started happening to the family that would change things forever. Aunt Jen died, Grandmother died, and things went to pieces. Jen was a neighborhood icon and her death affected the entire neighborhood. The church lost a leader of the Sunday School and the youth programs, the school PTA (Parent, Teacher Association) lost it leader, the local political ward lost one of its strongest community ward leaders, the City of Cleveland lost a faithful community leader with whom the politicians had fostered a great relationship, the Red Cross lost its area coordinator and we lost our mother. Cancer had taken her away.

Jen was so well liked her funeral was the biggest funeral since Bennie Madison the local gangster died. Jen's procession was over two hundred cars; city officials, school officials and teachers, church people, politicians, organizations with which she worked, friends and acquaintances. It was the beginning of the end of the days in the village.

My sister Barbara married and moved out. My Uncle began to date and I was considered in the way. Our relationship deteriorated. I moved out to live with another aunt after being told that I wasn't his son so he didn't have to take care of me. Soon after, I was kicked out of high school one month before graduation because of a disagreement with the new white Assistant Principal of the school whom I believed to have had a vendetta against me. The same man who fueled our argument by stating that the school had deteriorated since the colored students became dominant. While I was trying to give him evidence that the "colored" students had made the school better and more academically recognized in the city, he threatened to throw me out, and he did. My world seemed to be crumbling around me.

Back on E. 65th Street, our neighbors across the street was another family very close to ours. It was with the teenage daughter that I had my first real sexual experience. My Grandmother made "killer" bread pudding that was famous all over the neighborhood. My neighbor knew that Momma had made some bread pudding this day and I bargained with her to have sex with me for some of Momma's bread pudding. Sho' was good, sho' was good, the bread pudding I mean.

Next door to them was the McClarry's in the front house, and the Wilborn's in the back house off the alley. The two fine McClarry girls were popular in the neighborhood and I dated the youngest for a short time. Her older brother was a terrific baseball pitcher who played ball with one of the Wilborn boys in the back house, and my cousin Billy. All three boys from the neighborhood played on the same team, the Termites, and were all pitchers. Carl McClarry threw a baseball as hard as I ever saw any sandlot pitcher throw. I imagine he threw about one hundred miles an hour, easily.

Above the McClarry's were Mr. and Mrs. Smythe. Mr. Smythe was the neighborhood barber who tortured all of the little kids who were forced to sit in his chair while he clicked his false teeth. No matter what style you asked for, Mr. Smythe would cut it the same way every time, bald. If you asked for a Mohawk you would get bald. If you asked for dread locks; bald. I guess for fifty cents we couldn't complain.

Leonard Wilborn, my brother-in-law was the second part of the trio of pitchers, all of whom could have played in the major leagues if it hadn't been in the mid-fifties. Len was dating my sister and they were getting pretty serious when he was drafted to join the army. He and I had made a deal that I would watch out for other boys trying to move in on him. I must say I did a superb job having to defend my sister on several occasions from would be suitors. They married upon his release from the Army.

Back on our side of the street lived a family of girls named the Bradley's. Their father was one of the more colorful neighbors who could be heard singing the tune, "It's a Long Way to Tipperary" on any given Saturday night. I still don't know where Tipperary is. "Lucky" Bradley was around my age and was my friend.

In the same triplex lived the Madison family upstairs, Nate, Bobby, Jerome and James Arnold. These guys were good to have around because they all were good fighters and were pretty loyal to their friends. When other neighborhood crews would roll around on the block or in the playground where we played softball, it was comforting to know that the Madisons were there on your side.

Next to the Madisons lived the Tupper family. While I don't remember the girls in the family, I remember Monroe, the oldest boy, Tommy and Willie. Monroe was shot and killed by a white policeman while sitting in his car, unarmed. This is one of those things that make you know that you were once "colored". Being colored meant one thing to us and an entirely different thing to white people outside our village.

The last house on our side of the street was the James' house. I believe there were three girls and one boy. I remember Doris, the oldest girl, Carolyn, sexy, and a good cootie crawler, and Ernestine, the youngest. Eddie James was a good looking boy, and a good baseball player who also courted my sister. Incidentally, the Cootie Crawl was a kind of dance where you held a girl close and just grinded with her. Sometimes you would go to someone's basement party and the only light was a red bulb. When the slow records came on the whole bunch of kids would hit the floor and cootie crawl. You didn't take up much room because you didn't have to move out of one spot during the entire record. Whew! That was fun.

At the end of the block on our side was a church where most of the do woping took place. It was also here that Rudy and Three Finger Johnson, Black cops, would roust us for sitting on the church steps singing. We sang some of the most beautiful harmonies with Eugene Harkins leading that you would ever hear. Passers-by would stop and listen, occasionally join in, if we let them. We weren't disturbing anyone, maybe the cops; I guess they liked polka music or something.

Lastly, across the street from the church was Chapin's Service Station. The Chapin boys were some of the best baseball players on the whole east side of Cleveland and again, could have played major league baseball were it not for racism and prejudice. Otis was a first basemen and could tear the cover off a ball, Johnny was an outfielder who could run down any ball on his side of the field, and my bud Robert, a catcher, tough as nails and also a great hitter.

Well, that's a look at my neighborhood. A great place to have been raised. I'm sure that you must have had a neighborhood very similar to this one, if, when *you* were little you used to be colored.

Chapter 5

WHEN I WAS COLORED THE CHURCH was the center of our spiritual lives. Not only did we go to church on Sundays religiously, pun intended, we spent practically the whole day there. The ritual on Sunday morning was the same as long as I remember, getting up early, waiting for your turn to take a bath, unless you bathed the night before, getting dressed in your finest including your French toed shoes you got for Easter. Then you sat down for breakfast of toast and eggs or cereal. My Aunt liked bacon so we had the kind of bacon with the rind around the edges. I hated that because you had to pick the meat or fat from the rind.

Church was within walking distance of home and we all marched down the streets through the neighborhood looking all shiny and bright, meeting up with other children and parents also looking shiny and bright. While walking to church I met up with the neighborhood bully who loved to torment me. He was a stubby little boy who always hassled me when he was with his brothers. The two older boys would egg him on and this little turd would always throw me down and dirty up my shiny suit. This happened more than once and I vowed to get revenge one day.

Our church was a tiny little church by today's standards but seemed big to me when I was a kid. The nursery called the Cradle Roll was downstairs as was some Sunday school classrooms for the older kids and adults. The main hall where banquets and other programs were held was the center of the bottom floor. It was a huge room where we could run around and play after church services. At least it felt big then. Once a year the church would sponsor a dinner called "Everyone's Birthday" and every family brought food and cakes to share with everyone else. There were twelve tables set up; each one was a month of the year. I sat at May. This was a wonderful time because you sat with people you wouldn't normally sit with and break bread and share birthday cake after the great meals.

Upstairs was the chapel where the services took place and it was a large room with a balcony overhead. The Baptismal pool was on the pulpit along with a choir stand.

(Picture of Liberty Hill)

Our family which was rooted in the history of the church for many years before I was born occupied the balcony for the most part every Sunday. We, the kids, liked it because we thought we were isolated from the rest of the church and we could talk and have fun during the services. Apparently the minister and my Aunt Jen didn't quite hit it off and there was friction. I think the minister resented the fact that decisions about the church were always presented to my Aunt before to the minister. He was furious when that happened. It all came to a head one Sunday when one of our family got up during the sermon to go to the restroom and the minister screamed at them to sit down while he was talking. What was he thinking, because my Aunt waited until after the service and tore him a new one. After Jen died the minister had to be coerced to come to the wake and preach the funeral. It was soon after that that the minister retired.

Liberty Hill Baptist Church was a center of the community in the fifties. Its doors were open to the neighborhood kids and families with all kinds of activities from Summer Bible School to Boy Scouts and BTU, Baptist Training Union. All of the neighborhood ministers were leaders and spokesmen in the community and were respected by the families. When problems arose with the children or family members the minister was always called to help the family through. Many ministers lived on or near their church property.

Today it seems the central issues of the church are not the welfare of its members but the welfare of the church itself. Perpetuating the church institution is the job of the minister, community issues such as civil rights have been put aside until some issue arises that will result in publicity for the minister. They are not leaders but merely spokesmen.

I ran into an email not long ago that was entitled, "Raised in a Black Church". It was a test for Black people to determine if they have been to a black church, anywhere in America, and maybe even the Caribbean. The test asks certain question about words used during the service, usually by a church sister, who is making announcements during the Sunday service. This test is hilarious, not because what is says is so funny, but because what is said in the test is said in just about every Black church in America. Here's the test:

"First giving _____ to God, who is the _____ of my life, I'd like to say I'm glad to be in the _____ of the Lord one mo' time. Cause he brought me from a ___ long _____. I coulda been dead, sleeping in my _____, but God is _____ all the _____, and all the _____, God is _____. He's a _____ over troubled waters. He's a mother to the _____, and a _____ to the _____, a doctor in a _____ room, and a _____ in the courtroom! (smile) He's the_____ of the valley, a bright and _____ star He got up early one _____ mo'ning, with all _____ in his _____.

    Pray for me that I grow _____ in the Lord. Also, as you look in your church _____, under the special _____ please keep in your prayer _____ Sista Buela-Mae Jenkins who will be having her _____ surgery this week. And while you give your tithes and _____ we humbly ask that you contribute to the church _____ fund and we will be celebrating the pastor's fifteenth _____ so anybody please who serves on the _____ board please meet in the _____ following _____. And the women's auxiliary will be selling _____ dinners for $7.00 a _____ along with the youth _____ who will be having their annual _____ sale to help fund their trip to the national youth ministry _____ in Tennessee this summer. Parents please be _____ that vacation _____ school begins June 19. Please have your child _____ by May 13.

You knew them all, if not most of them, didn't you?!!! You must have gone to a Black church!

CHAPTER 6

ALTHOUGH OUR ELEMENTARY SCHOOL was segregated, we had a few white students and teachers. But the majority of the teachers were Black and each brought something of themselves to our lives to make themselves memorable. I'm sure you have memories of the teachers in your school. Let me talk first about the school, then the teachers afterward.

Wooldridge Elementary School sat on a hill right across the street from the Dan Dee Potato Chip factory. I think they put it there to torture us kids. That's alright because we got back at them by climbing the fence and stealing cans of potato chips in the evenings. Years later I realized that Dan Dee left those cans on their docks in plain view so that we could have them. A thoughtful gesture on their part.

Wooldridge was a large school with three floors of classes and a basement which housed the gymnasium and the restrooms. The floors were arranged so that the lower floor was the Kindergarten, first and second grades. The second floor was the third and fourth grades, the library and the music room. Between the second and third floor was a room at the head of the stairs where I learned French in the third grade. And, between the second and third floor on the other end of the building is where I learned to play trumpet. The top floor was for the big kids in the fifth and sixth grades. All of the classrooms were around the exterior walls so the middle of the building was open with a handrail around the entire circumference of the building. You could stand on the third floor and look straight down to the first floor.

I flunked Kindergarten. Now you think no one can do that. You're a baby for God's sake. What's there to flunk, nap time? Cookies and milk? Let me explain. The Cleveland schools divided the semester up into an A and B. You had to go through the B semester before you became an A student. So if you were a 4B you were in the first half of the fourth grade. A 4A student was in the last half of the fourth grade ready to move to the fifth grade. You could also start school in September or January. This worked because if your birthday was beyond September, you didn't have to wait until the next September to start school, you could start in January of that next year.

Well anyway, as you can imagine Cleveland is cold and often snowy in the winter. My Grandmother (Mama) would wrap me up in so many clothes that she was the only person who could figure out how to get to me. She would bring me to school every day and stay until *she* unwrapped me and removed my galoshes. Usually the Kindergarten teachers did this but my Grandmother didn't trust anyone to do this for her "baby". This pissed the teacher off so badly that she decided to flunk me to teach my Grandmother a lesson. So I repeated the Kindergarten because I wasn't mature enough to take off my own coat. And boots. I didn't care. That meant more milk and cookies and nap time for me. This was cool. What it really meant was that my peers with whom I started kindergarten were a semester ahead of me.

Somewhere along the way in my early years I was tested and determined to be in the upper levels in intelligence. This separated me out of the class into a group called the "Enrichment Class". This was a program in the Cleveland System which meant that the Enrichment Class was special and given more, education wise, than the other students. In later grades this became resentful for both teachers and regular students. We could walk down the halls and hear remarks such as "There goes the Enrichment Kid" or "Here come the Smarty Pants kids". And this was from the teachers.

This didn't bother me too much because I was very proud to be in the Enrichment Class. My sister and cousin had preceded me and it was an honor to follow in their footsteps. The Enrichment kids stayed together in one classroom, third, fourth, and fifth grades. The idea was that we third graders while having our own curriculum could also be exposed to the curriculum of the older kids. It was great. I learned a lot just listening to the older kids give their Morning Talks each day. One snowy, cold morning Ronald Cousins came running in the door of the classroom obviously late for his morning report because we were all sitting in a circle on the floor waiting. Ronald still had snow on his head and his coat dripping with water when he shouted "The Lion! The Lion, the King of the Jungle".

Our teacher was a beautiful lady named Louise Dayton Black; and as a ten year old I thought she was the most beautiful woman I had ever seen. Every morning we pledged allegiance to the flag and Mrs. Black would stand at the front of the class and hold her hand over her heart. Only she didn't let her hand touch her breast, she sort of arched it up like a salute. I watched her do that every day for three years waiting for her hand to touch her breast. It never did.

Mrs. Black was a great teacher who cared for the students and understood her role as leader of us special people. She was also a good disciplinarian in the days when teachers could whup your butt if you needed it. Mrs. Black didn't paddle us but her specialty was to bend your hand back and hit you with a ruler. Damn that hurt. It got our attention and it was not child abuse as the white folks named it, it was discipline. *Something that seems to be lacking today amongst our children.*

Our music teacher, Mrs. Merriman was also a beautiful colored woman with her flared hips and small waist. She was impeccably dressed everyday in her colorful sweaters. She taught us how to sing as a choir and what beautiful sounds we discovered because of her. We sang "Ava Maria" and "Waterboy" like a heavenly chorus, with Garfield Hayes as the lead singer. We sang at school assemblies and Parent Teachers Meetings, and we visited several other schools to perform.

"Water boy,
Where are you hiding?
If you don't come,
I'm gwonna tella yo mammy."

Sometimes we were exposed to the other teachers for special classes such as Social Studies or French. I started French in the third grade and it would continue through the ninth grade in Junior High. But one of the teachers we were exposed to was a teacher I'll call

Miss Cracker because that's what we called her in the third grade. I don't remember what she taught because the experience was such a horrible one. Miss Cracker was white and mean. She would throw chalk board erasers at the students, scissors, anything she could get her hands on. You talk about abuse, she believed in it. Once while in quiet time reading I needed to go to the restroom so I raised my hand to get her attention. She ignored me for the longest time. My bladder was full and I couldn't hold it much longer so I shouted out, "Miss Cracker I need to go to the restroom". She got angry at me and told me to sit there and shut up. Well, I sat there and peed on myself in front of the whole class. I never felt so humiliated in my short life. She sent me out of the room to the custodian downstairs who helped clean me up. I left school and went home. When I told my Aunt Jen what happened she became angry and stormed to the school to see the Principal. Mrs. Johnson, the Principal, called Miss Cracker in and my aunt climbed all over her explaining to her that if one of the students has to go to the restroom she best let them go. Jen's words carried weight because she was the President of the school PTA. I don't know what happened to Miss Cracker but I hope she found something else to do other than teaching. She obviously didn't like that, at least teaching colored kids.

Elementary school and the Enrichment Program had a profound effect on my early education. I attribute this experience to my success as an adult. I was exposed to so many things the normal students were not. I still see vividly images of that time. I was chosen to learn to play the trumpet in the third grade. I loved the instrument and continued to play until I attended high school and had to choose between music and sports. I chose sports. And, in that little room between the second and third floors I learned to speak French in the third grade.

For the sixth grade the enrichment students were amalgamated back into the school population and I was put into Mrs. Swollen's class. She was a little resentful of the enrichment kids and would often say to us, "You're just sitting there like a bump on a log". But I must say that I also remember her for the Banking experience in her class. Each Thursday morning Tellers from Society Bank would come to our class and teach us how to be bank tellers. We would actually set up a banking situation where the students could bring their ten or fifteen cents to our bank and we would log it into a regular savings account at the Society Bank. I still remember using a pen and ink to record the deposits into their bank books. Afterwards we would tally the money and the ledger to verify that they match and the Society Bank Tellers would take the funds to the bank. I still have my bank book somewhere today. That twenty cents that's in there is probably worth two million dollars today. Hmmm. I'd better find that book.

Oompa, Oompa, Oompa, Oompa
"Killi, Killi, Killi, Killi, wash, wash, wash, wash, keah, keah, keah.
Killi, Killi, Killi, Killi, wash, wash, wash, wash, keah, keah, keah.
Hail to Wooldridge School, her banner held up high.

This is what we had to sing at every assembly. I didn't have a clue then what it meant, and I still don't have a clue, but it was our fight song, and we shouted it at the top of our lungs. It's funny how I remember it and not my college fight song; that's probably because when I was in college I wasn't colored. And, it wasn't my village.

Chapter 7

I GOT "WHUPPED" EVERY DAY whether I needed it or not. About 3PM every day I was called into the house for my daily whupping. It got so bad that I would just check in about that time to see if someone had reported that I had done something worthy of a whupping. I wasn't a bad kid, just adventurous, bold and daring. I wasn't the kind of kid who waited for someone else to do something first, I did it first often to my detriment. When all of the children were given our allowance on Sundays, (fifty cents), we would head off downtown to a movie. We would hop the bus, pay 10 cents fare and get off a block from the movie theater. Most of the kids would hold hands and march along together. Not me. I was always finding something to explore along the way, whether it was an arcade through a building or through an alley. Coming home was the same. Very often I didn't ride the bus, I'd walk home exploring new neighborhoods and areas just to see what was there. As usual when I finally got home, sometimes hours after everyone else, my Aunt Jen would be waiting for me with her belt. She would hold one of my arms and whup me with her free hand. When I was little it hurt like Hell. But it didn't stop me. I still have that wondering spirit today, having lived in many places in the Western Hemisphere.

Once I was in the street in front of the house playing when I decided to lie down on the cobblestones on my belly and sing the song, "I Love You So Much It Hurts Me." I believe it was an Eddie Arnold song. But I wasn't just lying there singing, I was also grinding the cobblestones. My Aunt happened to hear me and see me gyrating in the street and called me inside. She asked what I was doing and I told her singing. Sometimes she could be so imaginative and I guess she was in the spirit because she asked me to lie on the living room floor and sing the song for her. She also asked me to do the little grinding thing I was doing outside. I knew this wasn't good when I saw the belt but I started singing and grinding on the carpet in the living room. The next thing I remember was a stinging sensation on my butt, over and over again. It lasted for what seemed like an eternity and when she was finished I laid there crying. Even though I felt abused at the time I really deserved that whupping. I had acted like an idiot in the street undoubtedly embarrassing my Aunt and she had whupped me. That worked a whole lot better than sitting me down having a discussion, or giving me a Time Out. I'm for discipline, it did hurt me then but it hasn't hurt me overall. What the Hell was I thinking?

CHAPTER 8

THERE WERE NO BASEBALL OR SOFTBALL DIAMONDS in our neighborhood because there wasn't any grass or space. So we had to play at the elementary school playground. Most of the time it would be available but if it wasn't the kids playing there would relinquish the field when we showed up because they knew we were going to play some serious softball. Our neighborhood was gifted with ball players and our family was especially gifted. Billy, the oldest of our family was the best softball player in the neighborhood, possibly the whole east side of Cleveland. Billy played shortstop and rarely missed a put out which he could reach. Billy was also a great baseball pitcher having struck out 24 batters in one game once when he played for the "Big Termites Baseball Team". He usually picked the players for the teams to play softball. I was probably one of the best all around athletes playing baseball, softball, basketball and football throughout high school. I was a pretty fair infielder and Billy and I made an awesome team when we played on the same team.

The playground was a gravel field when we first started playing, and we played football without pads. The football we played was tackle just like you see on Monday Night Football, but without pads or helmets. Chinch, a boy from a near-by neighborhood was the first guy to wear pads and a helmet. After that many of us wore pads and helmets that we bought from Salvation Army. The baseball diamond was also gravel and contributed to the fielding skills of Billy and myself. Dodging bad hops became a skill which saved you from getting your teeth knocked out when the ball hit a rock unexpectedly.

The outfield was restricted in left field by a set of swings, and seesaws in front of the building. The good hitters would knock the ball over the building on to the front lawn of the school. Most hitters would hit the ball to center field which was restricted by the building and its fire escape. The building was three stories tall in center field and the big hitters would rip one off the fire escape. But if you knew how to play the fire escape just right you could hold the runner to a double, maybe. Right field was the deepest part of the playground not having a building there just the side street. If you could hit it to right field you could get an inside the park homerun if you could run fast enough. We usually put our best outfielder in right field.

There was a sand box just off left field where Billy taught me how to slide into a base. He was the best base runner in the neighborhood and the best "hook slider" I've ever seen. We would spend hours just practicing in that sand box. Even today when I look at the major league games I can't see any of them sliding into second base like Billy could. Billy would slide and stand up at the end of the slide, like one motion. I never learned as well as Billy which resulted in a few "cherries" on my thigh after a baseball game as a "Little Termite team" or in high school. As a matter of fact, Billy taught me just about everything I knew back then.

We would spend hours practicing the "short hop" fielding skill. This is where we would intentionally throw the ball at each others feet so that you would have to catch it on the "short hop. This is the hardest ground ball fielding play in baseball and not everyone can do it. You have to understand the physics of what angle the ball will take when it gets to your glove or you could get hit in the mouth with the ball. It also was necessary for infielders to master for the throw from the outfield that came into second base or third base on one bounce. Billy or I never lost a tooth to a short hop.

One particular game sticks in my mind and has been there for fifty years. It's still vivid because Billy wouldn't let me forget it. This particular day we were playing a fierce game with all of the best players in our neighborhood there playing against a younger neighborhood team. Billy was at shortstop as usual and this time

I was playing left field. It was late in the game, getting dark when the other team was batting with the bases loaded and needed two runs to beat us. There were two outs in the last inning and the batter ripped one to left field and I could see that it was going to hit the building. What I didn't know until it got closer was whether it was going to hit high on the building out of my reach. I tip toed my way between the swings and the seesaws and timed my leap perfectly stretching until I heard the ball hit the pocket of my glove. The roar from the crowd was deafening, it had to be the greatest catch ever made in the playground's history and I made it. The batter was out and the game was over. All of my team mates congratulated me. All but one. Billy kept quiet during the celebration but unloaded on me afterward that I hadn't caught that ball, I had trapped it between my glove and the screen on the building window. You know jealousy is a hurting thing. He just had to take away my fifteen minutes of fame. That was fifty-five years ago and you know the first thing Billy said to me the last time I saw him? Yes, you're right. "Sonny, you know you didn't catch that ball, you trapped it off the window." Fifty-five years later and he still wouldn't let it go.

Billy carried his version of the "catch" to his grave, but I'm still hearing the roar of the crowd so that's my story and I'm sticking to it.

CHAPTER 9

REMEMBER WHEN I TALKED ABOUT THE BULLIES who used to throw me down on the way to church? Well if the truth be said, they used to meet me after school at the top of Beaver Hill and throw rocks at me or rough me up. I was a kid who could take care of himself but I knew fighting three brothers, one much bigger than me was foolish. So, I took the punishment until they moved out of the neighborhood. You see this today on TV or the movies and you say why doesn't he just knock the shit out of the bully, they usually will crumble at the first sign of defiance. That's easy to say. But when you see it on TV, it's not your ass that's being kicked.

Some people believe that revenge is sweet and others believe that it's best served cold. I say it's both of those. It was sweet and it was served cold, about three or four years cold.

One day at the playground while we were choosing sides for another great ballgame, guess who walks up with his two brothers asking to be chosen on one of the teams. You got it. W.B. the bully. Only four years later I'm 5'8" tall weighing 160 lbs. and W.B. and his brothers were still about 5'1" or 5"2". When I saw them the first thing I did was laugh out loud. Billy caught on and we both laughed out loud. Billy knew what was coming next and I didn't disappoint him. I grabbed W.B. in the collar and punched him square in his mouth. I threw his ass down on the ground where he lay whimpering. I reached for his brothers and they both hauled ass out off the playground leaving W.B. to fend for himself. I must have remembered the third passage that says, "Revenge is mine sayeth the Lord" because I couldn't hurt him anymore. He was crying like a baby thinking that I was going to kick his ass all over that playground, so I let him up and he took off across the playground until he turned around the building and disappeared. That was the last time I saw the bullies. It did feel good though. Nature sometimes plays cruel tricks on people.

That playground behind that elementary school was a social development program for our neighborhood and it didn't cost the tax payers a dime. It was there that the greatest cadre of baseball, basketball, and football players in Cleveland was raised, and learned such principles as fair play and sportsmanship. We weren't threatened by the gangs as kids because we were too busy playing sports against other neighborhood even, and having a world of fun. And the only reason some of us didn't make the big leagues was because of the same old bullies that I'm still fighting, racism and discrimination.

CHAPTER 10

Before the Government took over gambling on the lottery, there was the numbers. This was a game where people would pick certain numbers and if those numbers were pulled over in the alley behind our street, you could win a lot of money. That is if the numbers runner paid off which they did not sometimes. And if they didn't, who were you going to tell, Ghost Busters? You couldn't go to the police because the game was illegal, you couldn't hassle the numbers runner because he was connected to the mob running the game. You were just SOL as they say.

Once in a while the Police would raid the numbers game which was held in the alley. The numbers guys would pull a ball from a paper bag or a bingo basket similar to the Lotto ball and that's how you won. If you matched the numbers, just like the lotto, you would win. There were a lot of people standing around waiting for the numbers to be called when the police would try to sneak up on the game. There were numbers lookout everywhere and when they saw a police car they would holler "Raise" as loudly as they could and the gangsters would shut the game down, and everyone would scatter in all directions. I don't remember if anyone was ever caught and I think that was the way it was planned, if you know what I mean.

Every now and then you would see a lady walking up our street who was unfamiliar to us. She was usually wearing some doughty outfit so as to not call attention to herself so she thought. She was usually carrying a shopping bag, large purse on her arm or a shoebox and walking fast. This was the bag lady taking the cash and the slips from the game to the boss. Occasionally she wouldn't make it and would end up dead somewhere and her shopping bag missing. That was why they used different women who used different routes to deliver the money. Part of life in the colored neighborhood.

Chapter 11

ONE THING ABOUT BEING POOR, you have to be creative. Children are very creative when it comes to entertaining themselves. We didn't have the latest gadgets or toys, sometimes we didn't have any toys at all. We nailed two sticks together to make a gun to play cowboys and Indians, or, we crushed tin cans on our feet to make can shoes to clang around the street, or when we were older, we made skatemobiles out of fruit crates and old steel roller skates. One of the most fun things we made were stilts from old two by fours. Some kids didn't have the balance to walk on stilts, but if you did it was fun. If we did have toys they had been bought from the Salvation Army, cheaply.

Practically all of your activities were outside, even in the winter. If you weren't studying or reading for school, you were outside. So we had to create games to occupy our time. Most all of the kids played Marbles because we had marble contests at school playing against other schools. My Aunt Jen believe it or not was a marble champion having competed as a child at school. It must have run in the family because we were pretty good ourselves. You could always tell the good shooters because we had the biggest bag of marbles or we carried them in a cigar box. I remember having to fight my way out of someone's yard more than once because I won all of their marbles.

We played a game called "Chubby". Since childhood I have found that other colored kids in other cities played a similar game called, "Root-a-Peg" or some other name. It was called Root-a Peg because at the end of the game, the loser had to root the peg, which means you had to dig the knife or ice pick out of the dirt with your mouth. I have played it with a kitchen butter knife and a switch blade; whatever you have is generally ok.

The smart players also carried a piece of leather or a folded sheet of paper so that the blade of your weapon of choice didn't puncture your hand. Boy, I can still taste the dirt in my front yard.

My sister Barbara was one of the best Roly Poly players I had ever seen. This was a game the girls generally excelled at more than the boys, although we tried to be good at it. All you needed for this game was a flat sidewalk, two squares, a ball, and a piece of chalk. The game board looked like eight squares numbered from one to eight. The idea was to roll the ball in square one and step into it with one foot. Then you bounce the ball once in all eight squares. Then you roll the ball into square two, step in boxes one and two, catch the ball before it crosses the lines, step in each square bouncing the ball twice in each square and so on and so on. Sounds simple? When you get to squares five through eight you really have to have touch, "terch" as some of the kids called it to keep the ball inside the square until you step into all of the previous squares. Now try that and see how easy this game is. My sister probably hasn't played this game in over fifty years but I'd still put my money on her today. I don't think I could get down that low anymore to catch the ball. It would take me all day to get to two.

I was never the fastest kid in the neighborhood, I wasn't even near the top ten fastest kid, but I loved to run and for my age group I could hold my own. This was especially important when we set up the relay races. If you could just hold the position for your team and not get "chopped down" you would get chosen on a team. We would pick three of four teams and station the relay all around 65th Street and 67th Street. We ran in the middle of the street unless a car pushed you off to the side on or on to the sidewalk. We always put our fastest runners at the first position and the last position. This way if you could get a lead you could hand off to a slower runner who only had to keep the lead until you could make the baton pass to your anchor man who was the fastest kid on your team. We had some awesome races, even though you couldn't see the race on the other block unless your ran through the yards to see the runners passing by, but to see a runner come around the corner at the end of the block was like watching Jesse Owens winning the four by one hundred relay in the 1939 Olympics. You wouldn't know who would round the corner first but the baton was passed at the end of the street and your anchor man had to bring it home. If the hand off was made to either Eugene or Willie, you could forget it unless they were on your team. Eugene was about 6'3", lanky with a great stride, and Willie was a track star in school. Watching either one of them was as entertaining as watching the Olympics on television today. This was our Olympics.

Of all the street games we played I think that "Set Back" was my favorite. My favorite because I was one of the better players in the neighborhood. This game was not for the weaklings and only a few could qualify to play. Some of the greatest players in the neighborhood besides myself, were Howard, Eugene, and Calvin (June) Wilborn, the brother of my Brother-in—Law. The only equipment needed to play this game was a rubber ball. The game stared with two teams standing in the middle of the street. There was no rule as to how many players but you didn't need many. Only the strongest arms you could find. The object of the game was to throw the ball over the heads of the opposing team until one team was backed up against the cross streets at the head-end or back-end of the block. We had some good strong arms on our street and I was fortunate to be one of the strongest. But I couldn't hold a candle to June Wilborn. He was tall and lanky and had long arms that looked like it wound up so far behind his back it touched the ground behind him, and uncoiled to touch the ground in front of him when he threw the ball. June was by far the best thrower in our neighborhood. If this was an Olympic sport, I'd bet that June could make the team. It never happened but I believe if there had been a contest between Rocky Colavito of the Cleveland Indians who could stand at home plate and throw a baseball into the stands in center field, and June Wilborn, neighborhood colored kid, it would have been close.

If it sounds like we had fun when we were colored, we did. Remember we didn't have television until we were young teenagers and there were probably only one or two of them in the neighborhood. There were no electronic games to keep us occupied for hours like the kids today, and only a few teenagers had access to cars so we were pretty much confined to our neighborhood and the surrounding neighborhoods. We played together, we lived together, we looked out for each other, and it was a village. It was a neighborhood not just a residential area.

CHAPTER 12

BACK WHEN I WAS COLORED there was no drug problem per se. What we had were a few people in the neighborhood who we called Dope addicts and drunks. As a matter of fact, we knew the names of the people who were the addicts and drunks. They never bothered anyone, no one tried to emulate them, and they were the outcasts of the neighborhood. These people were usually hooked on Heroin and got their supply of drugs from secret places not known to us. They were in a world all their own. Of course the neighborhood drunks were our fathers or brothers or neighbors down the street. They were for the most part harmless and we viewed them as funny. When Mr. Bradley staggered down the street drunk on Saturday night singing "It's a Long, Long Way to Tipperary" we laughed because it was funny. Mr. Bradley was going home and would most likely fall asleep once he got there. And, he was walking. Not driving putting others in danger. I would be naïve to think that no one in the neighborhood took drugs or didn't drink a little too much from time to time, but you weren't exposed to it in school or on the street as you are today. Sure, we had characters like Dirty Dan the Reefer Man who sold marijuana to the older folks but he was the only name I remember actually in the drug trade. And you either had to drive around in another neighborhood to find him or make a connection through someone else who had access to the drug. It was considered rare when you came into contact with the drug trade. We had many house parties in those days and there was no drug problem associated with those parties. Sometimes the kids smuggled wine or booze into a party but again it was the exception, not the rule.

When as teenagers we discovered how to buy booze illegally, it would take us all day to gather enough coins together, go to the designated fake gas station, roll down the car window, tell the attendant what we wanted, hand him the money and he would deliver our order to the car. If one of the kids drank too much we would try to sober him up before we took him home because you didn't want to take him home drunk. The next day your parents would get a call and the drunk's parent might be calling to tell your parents that you were with their son or daughter last night, drinking. We had to sneak to drink or smoke weed. If you were caught doing it in your parents home, you could be beat to within an inch of your life. And there was no such thing as a kid selling drugs that was only for the gangsters on the street or in certain houses. God was alive and living in our parents and grandparents who believed in not sparing the rod.

CHAPTER 13

OUR HOUSE HAD WHAT WE THOUGHT was a huge backyard, in fact we played baseball in it. Although the outfielders had to stand on the other side of the detached garages behind the house, we managed to play some pretty good games there. At night the yard would turn into something else. It became my private viewing area to spy on Nappy, the Prostitute. Nappy's house was directly behind mine but her address was on East 67th Street. Her back bedroom window faced our backyard. Nappy was an attractive woman, at least to a young teenage boy suffering through puberty. The older boys said she was a prostitute, I don't really know if this was true or if they were trying to impress the younger me. Every day Nappy and her sister would walk through my yard to get to the back of her house. I would always rush to the window or the door to see Nappy switch her generous butt through the yard. Nappy was also endowed with large breasts which she would display in sweaters and low cut dresses.

At night, Nappy would conveniently leave her shade just a few inches up in her bedroom facing my yard and I would sneak a look in her window occasionally when I thought she was changing clothes. I got lucky a few times and saw her undress in front of her mirror. She was a beautiful woman by my teenage standards and I still believe she lingered in the nude until she thought I had enough pleasure time. I am sure she knew I was there because she would pull the shade down when her show was over. Her name was not Nappy; I named her that after viewing the curly hair around her private area. This became a joke between my buddy and me with whom I shared my private viewing gallery occasionally.

I am embarrassed by this now but as a young teenager I enjoyed the experiences. As many teenagers experience, my hormones were raging almost all of the time. Nappy was a welcome relief.

CHAPTER 14

ONE OF THE NASTIEST INSECTS AROUND IS THE ROACH. They are quiet, quick and hard to catch. Our house from time to time was infested by these little creatures and we, the kids, would stage roach wars to rid the house of the pests. This was either before Orkin or they just didn't work in our neighborhood. Even if they did my folks couldn't afford their service, so we took it upon ourselves to exterminate them.

Roaches are sneaky and generally only show up when the lights are out and you're not around. Occasionally one would wonder out when you were around and of course he was dead, if you could catch it. We had tried different methods such as roach motels and stuff like that and that would work for a short period in a small area. But to really make an impact we declared war on them. War meant getting at least two push spray cans filled with Black Flag Roach Poison, removing the dishes and glasses from the cabinets and sprinkling a little sugar in the cabinets. One warrior would stand on one side of the cabinet and the second warrior would stand on the opposite side of the cabinet. After a period of time a third person would turn the lights on and the war was on. Roaches would run around and head for their exit points and you had to be fast to cut them off with spray. If you were successful, you could kill hundreds of roaches especially after they became disoriented from the poison. If a few tried to get away by another route, you had to spray that area which would turn them around where you could get a clear shot at them. While you were spraying the roaches you had to talk to them or make that movie background music like in the war movies. This made it fun.

49

You'd be surprised how many roaches you could kill during a war, particularly if you could discover a nest and spray that area. That wasn't easy to do sometimes because once the lights came on the roaches would head for any crack they could find and disappear. Your only hope was for the surviving roaches to take the poison back to the nest on their bodies to contaminate the eggs or other roaches. It usually worked and your home was roach free for a period of time. After the roach wars we had to make sure that we took precautions with food crumbs lying around and dishes left in the sink and emptying the trash regularly. But it seemed that no matter how much hygiene you practiced the roaches would eventually come back. Partly because the houses were so old they could hide in the walls and/or come into your house from a near by house that hadn't had a war in some time. Oh! But you don't know what I'm talking about, let me move on.

Chapter 15

YOU ONLY NEED ONE WORD to evoke the fondest memories of our family in the forties and fifties, Jen. Jen was undoubtedly the head of our family, the whole family whether you lived in Cleveland, Pittsburgh, Cincinnati, or Alabama. Jen was the most brilliant person I knew. Only possessing a high school education, Jen could have lectured at any university in America on family life, organizational skills, politics and love. Jen was my mother's older sister and the third oldest of seven children. She was rail thin standing about 5'9", a giant to a small child. In many ways Jen was a giant. She had her hands in everything in the church serving as Sunday School Superintendent for years, in the community, serving as PTA President during our school years, in politics as Ward Chairman and Committeeman for many years, and mother and mentor to six children (including my sister and me) of her own, and dozens of others in our community. My sister and I had lived with our Aunt Jen for all of our pre-school and school day lives and she was really the only mother we knew. Thank God for extended families. That happened a lot when I used to be colored.

Our house was the center of activity in the neighborhood and our front porch served as the gathering place for every child who wanted to come by, sit, listen to stories by Melvin, do wop with Eugene, spit shine your combat boots with Howard and the older teenagers, or talk about the fantastic catch I made at the playground with Billy (I just threw that in). The kids knew that there was a second home at Jen's. Jen's influence stretched from E. 69th Street to East 61st Street, bordered by Woodland Avenue on the north, Beaver on the south, and Kinsman on the west and southwest.

Before there were computers, Jen taught us how to research information and material for school and pleasure. We spent time reading encyclopedia, magazines and library books. Jen's caring and influence followed me long after her death through high school and college. Being the first college graduate in the family, I have to thank Jen for my accomplishment. Although there were many who influenced my development no one had as much influence as Jen.

Now there are some things about Jen that were not quite peaches and cream, at least as a child I didn't think so. One of those questionable things was why I got spanked almost every day, why I had to watch and help Jen prepare Sunday and holiday meals, and why I had to wear homemade underwear fashioned from old pants. I didn't understand then but guess what? I'm a much better person for the spankings which I deserved, I love to cook and was written up in an Idaho Newspaper for my Quiche Lorraine recipe, and I understand the value of a dollar. What a visionary she was.

IN MEMORIUM

Mrs. Jeannette Drake Jones

1912 — 1955

My mother's oldest brother was Robert, simply known as "Buck". I bet every family has a colorful uncle who is memorable. His name may be Uncle Skip, or Bobby, or Leroy, but no matter what their name was they were characters. My Uncle Buck lived in Chicago, alone, in a small apartment with seven latches and locks on his door. He said that people were after him and he needed to protect his space. Once he told me that someone put a snake in his bed and that's why he needed a lot of door locks. It was hard to know when you could believe Buck so you just listened and said, "Oh yeah?"

Uncle Buck wore his pants above his ankles and a belt that sat on the top of his big belly, and would only come to Cleveland around Christmas time and just happened to show up Christmas Day after the presents had been opened. Usually one of the kids had gotten a game such as checkers, darts, or monopoly and Uncle Buck would set us up. He would pretend to show us how to play the game then coax us to bet our few pennies on the game. Well, you know the outcome; Buck would win the money and split. He would take our money and leave us crying.

Watching Uncle Buck eat dinner was not for the faint of heart or stomach. Your food would get cold because you would be watching Buck. If the meal consisted of chicken, Mashed potatoes, green beans, and yams, Buck would take his fork and mix all of these ingredients together on his plate so that it looked like he was eating garbage. Then he would eat it with his "pinkie" sticking up in the air like royalty. After every bite of his garbage Buck would take the napkin and wipe the corners of his mouth. You had to be there to fully appreciate the picture I'm trying to illustrate here. It might take him an hour to eat his food with his special technique. So you had to concentrate on your own meal or get up and leave the table with your food, or you could starve to death just watching his antics.

Neither my aunt, uncle nor grandmother drank alcohol so our house was fairly conservative and quiet, except when Uncle Berlin, whom we called Uncle B, came over. Uncle B was always a source of entertainment because he liked to play around with us kids when he came. The only problem was that Uncle B was always drunk when he came around. Once when we were playing in the basement which was coal bins and a dirt floor, Uncle B, drunk, decided he wanted to play whatever it was we were playing. We gladly let Uncle B join in and as he was playing at the top of the stairs he tripped and fell all the way down the stairs to the basement floor. We thought that was the funniest thing we had ever seen and just laughed and laughed. Uncle B was lying at the bottom of the stairs moaning and cussing when we came over to where he lay and said in our giggling voices, "Do it again Uncle B, do it again". Well, Uncle B didn't play fair, he quit the game and left. We continued without him, he just didn't know what fun he was missing.

Chapter 16

LIFE IN THE GHETTO WAS HARSH at times and we experienced it from time to time. Several times the telephone was cut off for lack of payment but that didn't impact us as kids and much as it did the adults. Since all of our friends and relatives lived in or near the neighborhood we could just go to their houses to communicate. No phone, big deal. Funny thing, you could get a call but you couldn't call out. This was because of the "party line" where someone else shared the line.

My aunt and uncle did the best they could to make ends meet but with six children and three adults in the house, that was sometimes a tall order that couldn't get filled. I remember when we got a piano, a player piano at that. I don't know where it came from but we really enjoyed pretending we could play. My sister Barbara could play and was taking lessons on the piano. Cleveland has harsh winters and for about three to four months you need heat. Well, one of those tall orders was to keep the heat on for the children to stay warm. This particular winter the city turned the heat off for lack of payment and my uncle brought a pot belly stove into the house, vented it through the wall to outside, and provided heat from coal, or wood or whatever could burn. The *whatever could burn* turned out to be the player piano. It was sad to see the piano get dismantled piece by piece to provide heat in the stove but you have to do what you have to do to provide for your family. It got us through the winter.

I didn't know this at the time, but I'd bet my bottom dollar that our family was not the only one having difficulty paying its bills. My aunt and uncle worked at steady jobs and it was still hard for us to make it through the winter each year. A steady job to a colored person was a job with the lowest classification and wage. My aunt worked for white people washing and ironing and taking care of their children for minimum wages at best. But we were never on welfare or ADC (Aid to Dependent Children).

Poor or not we always had food to eat. Whether it was potted meat or fried chicken, we always seemed to have enough to go around. The main cooks in the house were my Aunt Jen, my Grandmother and my sister. As I recall our menu hardly ever varied from week to week. Basically we were raised on the same food through out our school years. Mondays were Neck Bones or Lima beans; Tuesdays were meatloaf and mashed potatoes, Wednesdays were spaghetti or chili; Thursdays were pot roast or beef stew; Fridays were my favorite meals of macaroni and cheese and fish; Saturdays were usually Kosher wieners and pork and beans or cream style corn. Once in a while, which suited me just fine; Grandma would drag out her pressure cooker and put some Chitlins on. That day the house smelled like - - - - and we would always have to clean the Chitlins off the ceiling because Grandma would blow up the pressure cooker. I'm sure it wasn't always but it seemed that way to me. I never learned to appreciate the taste of those morsels even today.

Sunday was a special day around the house. Dinner was a grand affair which had been started on Saturday night. Watching my aunt and peeling the potatoes or boiling the eggs, or stirring the sweet potato pie mix was my job. Sometimes I made the crusts for the pies cutting in the Crisco in the flour and rolling the dough into the pie pans. After awhile I got pretty good at this and it turned from drudgery into a fine art. I'm a pretty good cook today because of the lessons I learned watching My aunt, grandmother and sister when they prepared food for the daily and Sunday dinners.

Either fried chicken or ham was the main dish and it would be served after church service. Our relatives from all over the neighborhood would come to Jen's on Sunday for dinner. The Rudolphs, the Fileys and the Drakes would meet at Jen's often bringing with them cakes or pies for dessert. You saw this tradition on the TV show "Soul Food" if you watched it. I think most families did this when we were all colored. Now that we are African Americans I'm not sure it still happens, at least not as much. Families are so spread out now, even living in different cities today. Ah! Those were the days.

You know when you're poor you have to do a lot of stuff rich people don't have to do. Take bottles back to the store to get your penny deposit. That was embarrassing pulling your wagon down the street with everyone looking. The whole neighborhood knew then that your family didn't have any money that week. It really didn't embarrass us, but we thought it did. Most of our neighbors did the same thing from time to time.

Eating potted meat and neck bones, even chicken feet was regular fare in our house. I don't know any white folks who ate chicken feet.

Poor people also remember playing in the dirt, in the front yard, if you had a front yard. There was no such thing as a lawn or a lawn mower. You swept your yard with a broom when it became littered with leaves or paper and debris.

CHAPTER 17

MY AUNT USED TO MAKE US WEAR home made "underwear". Now I know you rich white folks don't know anything about home made underwear. My aunt, having six kids to raise couldn't afford to buy new underwear every year, so she would make it from old pants. She would cut off the legs of the old pants up near the crotch and tear the pockets out. The one thing she didn't do was take the zippers out so when you had to go to the toilet, you had to unzip twice before you could pee. You would pray that zipper number two didn't get stuck or you were—out of luck; which happened to me a few times. And you basically were wearing two pair of pants so you looked real puffy around the middle.

There are dozens of stories to be told about being poor, but the one I like the best is the one I call Voo-voo Flap. Now some of you former poor people may remember this.

Every fall we would go to a local children's clothing store and get new pants for school. Being raised in Cleveland, the new pants would be some cheap material that would keep you warm during the winter such as corduroy, heavy wool or denim. Some times you even got a new pair of cheap shoes that was supposed to last the entire winter. Well, I was a pretty rough-house kid who played basketball, baseball, and football in these shoes so they didn't last very long. The sole would be the first to go and my aunt would glue the sole back on, but after a few more games of basketball the sole would come apart again. This time you would have to wait your turn before the shoes were taken to the shoe shop to be repaired. So, in the meantime you had to walk around in those raggedy shoes and your new corduroy pants. You sounded like a one man band when you walked to school and back. Your corduroy pants would make the voo-voo sound when your thighs would rub together, and your raggedy shoes would make the "flap" sound each time you took a step. So all the way to school you would hear "voo-voo flap", voo-voo flap", "voo-voo flap". We named those corduroys, "whistle britches". Come to think of it we could have used this rhythm as background for a rap tune.

CHAPTER 18

AS A CHILD I WAS SOMEWHAT aware of the differences between colored life and white life but it was not so much based on race, I thought is was just the way it was. I lived in the ghetto and white children lived in the suburbs. I'd seen the way they lived when a gang of us would take our shovels and ride the bus to the suburbs to shovel snow for a quarter a yard. Beautiful houses and yards and white kids who didn't have to shovel, just watched us from their windows do the work. The differences were magnified when we saw television and especially the commercials where white women dressed in bright clothes just to mop the beautiful floors in their beautiful homes, or stand at the door and wave goodbye to their men going off to work in suits and ties and wide brimmed felt hats.

I thought the most beautiful houses in the world were those houses we shoveled snow from the 200 feet driveways in Shaker Heights. The houses, mansions, were huge white siding mansions with black Shutters on the windows; maybe one hundred windows, or so it seemed. The roofs were black asphalt shingles which set the house off even more than the dozens of trees, mostly pine, around the property. The lawns were so big you could play Hide the paddle, or It and never be found just hiding behind those massive trees. The grass, yes grass, in the yards looked like it had been carpeted with each blade the same height.

In the winter the grass would be so white and pure looking you would think it was painted by Thomas Kinkade. There were no footprints or car tracks or anything on the snow. The pine trees would catch the snow on its branches and if you looked long enough at a tree you could see a blob of white snow fall from a branch when the sun was shining and melting the snow high up in the trees. I wondered how it looked from inside the mansion. Breathe taking I bet. I bet those white children looking at me work so hard to clean their driveway never gave this scene a single thought. Just remembering how beautiful Shaker was when I was a kid reminds me of the poem, Stopping By Woods on a Snowy Evening, by Robert Frost. The first paragraph of the poem describes the scene perfectly to me:

"Whose woods these are I think I know,
His house is in the village though;
He will not see me stopping here
To watch his woods fill up with snow."

Chapter 19

IT TOOK ME A FEW YEARS to figure it out but my good friend Carl, a white child, moved out of the neighborhood when we finished elementary school and I never saw him again. I didn't understand until later when I put it together. Carl's parents didn't want to send him to a predominantly colored school for his early teen years; they wanted Carl to be with other white kids, doing things that white kids did, in a safer environment, she thought. It was kind of like re-segregation which I understand.

It wasn't until I was a mid-teen that I had my first real brushes with racism and discrimination. I played organized baseball on a team called the Little Termites, and our team played all over Cleveland. We played against white teams and experienced the usual racist cat calls and racial slurs from the white players and the audiences but we usually won so it made it more tolerable. I still have the two inch scar on my left thigh put there by a white boy sliding into second base during a game. Besides, we weren't civil rights leaders we were kids having a good time. But this luxury came to a screeching halt when I heard the news about a colored kid named Emmett Till who had been murdered by two white men in Money, Mississippi in 1955, who were later acquitted of murder and kidnapping by all-white juries. People across America were outraged, at least colored people were, and it affected me in a way that would stay with me for the rest of my life. In fact later on in life I would become very active in the Civil Rights Movement because of it.

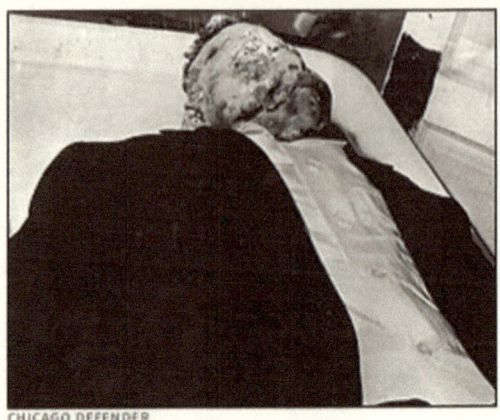

CHICAGO DEFENDER

Jet Magazine showed pictures of the badly battered body and face of this young boy from Chicago and the only thing I could think of was revenge. Not just for Emmett Till but for all of the transgressions reaped upon our people that I had basically overlooked as a young man. I was becoming of age and of understanding. This new fire burning inside of me was so intense it drove me to make plans to travel to Mississippi to seek revenge. I had no idea what I was going to do there, probably become a victim myself, but I wanted to hurt white people in retaliation. I actually discussed going there with my aunt who talked some sense into my head. She also showed me how I could do more good if I stayed in school and became a person who could effect change doing positive things for my people. I did calm down as far as running away to Mississippi, but the fire continued to burn, although in a more controlled manner.

We now have the Jena 6 trials in Louisiana and Travon Martin in Florida which are so mindful of the Emmett Till injustice that it too may serve to awaken the spirit of the colored people in America to regain that fire and persistence we exhibited during the Civil Rights Movement of the sixties and seventies. The air is just as heavy with the weight of America's sins today as it was when we grieved for Emmett. We all need to become *colored* again. When I was working in the Movement in the sixties an old Black man said to me when I talked about Afro-Americans that "*We have always been colored and we will always be colored. Don't call me Afro-American*". Was this old man a prophet?

Chapter 20

CLEVELAND WAS ALWAYS GETTING HIT by tornadoes when I was a kid. It seemed like every couple of years a huge tornadoes would hit the city and some trailer park would disappear along with some person or a bunch of cars. But you know, the tornadoes would always miss the east side of town where most of the colored people lived and hit the west side hard, where the white folks lived. Every time there was massive damage it would happen to some white folks on the west side, while only a few trees would get broken on our side of town. I remember once when a white insurance man was visiting our neighborhood collecting all of his 10 cents policies when the tornado hit and the big tree in our front yard fell on top of his car. This was the only damage to the neighborhood, his car and our tree. A coincidence? I think not. Justice, it was justice pure and simple. It comes in different ways. We'll take it any way we can get it.

When I reported to work at a federal government facility I was told I needed a security clearance. I was introduced to the head of Security who was a Herbert Hoover wanna be. He actually believed that he should have succeeded Hoover as head of the FBI. He escorted me to a small room in the facility where we were supposed to review my application. The first question this racist asked was why I had lied on my Personal Security Questionnaire. This made me more nervous than I already was being in this little room with a racist white man with a gun and I asked him to what was he referring. His response was "You didn't put down any arrest record." Now I was a grown-assed man and he pissed me off. But I knew I had to maintain so that I could get badged to work there. I told him that I didn't have an arrest record, and he said, "That's unusual, all Negroes had arrest records". This is no joke. He really said that. Then he said you didn't put down where your father is buried, which was one of the questions on the clearance form. I answered that I don't know where my father is buried since I never knew my father. He turned red as a beet and started to rant about my lying on the form and I was not going to get my clearance and what was I hiding, and on and on. To make a long story short, I reported him and I finally received my clearance from the Federal Government.

I tell this story to lead into the story of my first bicycle. My Aunt and Uncle raised my sister and me from the time we were infants. Thank god for the "extended family" practiced by so many colored people then. The only time we saw our mother was sometimes at Christmas when she would travel to Cleveland from her home in Cincinnati. I never knew my father and I was told that I met him when I was about three or four years old. Motherdear, as we called our biological mother, would always bring gifts such as clothes for school, etc.

During my eighth birth year Motherdear asked me what I really wanted and I responded, a bicycle. I thought no more about it and life went on after her visit was over as usual. On my eighth birthday when I got home from school, there was a beautiful red and cream colored bicycle sitting in the living room of the house. It was my birthday gift from my mother. I was thrilled and excited, so excited I immediately took the bike outside and mounted it proudly about to take my very first ride down the street. I knew I wasn't allowed to ride in the street so I stayed on the sidewalk peddling at what seemed like a hundred miles an hour. The bike had a horn mounted in the crossbar side panels and as I approached a man walking in my path I blew my horn, and blew my horn and the man didn't move. I panicked and ran into the man's butt. The front wheel of my brand new bike went between the man's legs and he buckled like he was going down, and I flew off the bike into the street. The man must not have been hurt so he turned his attention to me bending down to help me up from the street. My brand new bicycle was lying on its side with the front wheel spinning. I wasn't really hurt either except my heart was broken as I saw the front fender of my brand new bike twisted and bent lying to one side of the wheel. My very first ride on my brand new bike had been a disaster. I felt like I was going to die right there. I cried, not because I was injured but because I was feeling the pain of my heart being broken. Well I survived obviously but that was the first time that I remember feeling heart broken and hurt. Life was to afford me other instances and like my new bike I learned to get over it and keep on trucking. I never told my mother and I don't think she ever found out about my birthday disaster.

Chapter 21

SATURDAY NIGHT WAS A NIGHT of great anticipation because we could watch this new phenomenon call television. Radio with a picture and Bunny would let us kids watch the John Wayne Theater. This is before John Wayne stood in a boxing ring on television and proclaimed that Negroes are the cause of their own problems and need to pull themselves up by their bootstraps. I think is the first time I heard that expression. Even though old John was partly right what he failed to accept was that racial discrimination was the major cause of our sufferings, and we didn't have any bootstraps to grasp on to. His remarks also helped to fuel the Civil Rights Movement. But I digress.

Bunny's TV as it was called, was the first in the neighborhood and was seven inches across. But you know it seemed like a movie screen to us and it was probably 15 kids gathered around this TV at one time. Then Bunny, who must have been the neighborhood innovator, created the first color television in the neighborhood. He put a piece of plastic across the screen with a blue stripe, a red stripe, a green stripe, and a purple stripe running horizontally. Color TV. Wow! We were lucky kids. Bunny didn't stop there. When color TV was created in Bunny's house the word spread and the crowds increased, so Bunny had a solution for that. He bought a big piece of glass that magnified the picture from seven inches to about twelve. It didn't matter that we now couldn't make out any images because it was so blurred; we had large screen color TV in the neighborhood and loved it. Who said being colored didn't have its advantages?

Years later we had TV in our house also. Our black and white screen was about 14 inches and it changed our lives drastically. Up until this time we didn't know we were poor. We didn't know there was something better across town. Television showed us that. We hardly ever saw a colored person on TV until Nat King Cole got his own show, Rochester, the Servant took care of Jack Benny's house, and Amos and Andy became the funniest show on TV.

Then it happened. The Colored people began to turn into something else. Negroes. Amos and Andy became an embarrassment, Rochester and Steppin Fetchit become symbols of the slave mentality, and Kingfish became a symbol of a "fool". We were told to protest those images and demand more images such as Jackie Robinson, Larry Doby, Ralph Bunche and George Washington Carver. The transformation began as we made demands for respect. We were even told not to accept the term "colored" anymore. We were Negroes seeking better jobs, better housing, better education and "integration". We truly would not be the same. The world would not be the same.

Being a Negro now I thought it would be different but I found out that nothing really changed except what I was called. I still lived in the ghetto, on the same old street, with the same rats and roaches I lived with when I was little. Even though I was sixteen years old and the oldest child still at home. Billy, and Barbara had married and moved out and my uncle and I weren't getting along very well. I was trying to look out for the younger children in the house and my uncle was trying to start a different phase of his life, moving on.

My grandmother had been moved to my Aunt Lee's to live and she was beginning to show signs of Dementia so she had to be watched all the time. My Aunt Lee would watch her during the day and I volunteered to watch her after high school football and basketball practices. Mama was also going blind from diabetes and this brought on depression. One day after school I got to Aunt Lee's house just after Lee had left for work Lee's husband, Johnny was in the yard painting signs for his customers, and I found Mama kneeling in the kitchen in front of the oven, with her head inside the oven. Mama was trying to kill herself by turning on the gas and asphyxiating herself. Luckily, she didn't turn on the right button.

Back at home, I asked my uncle if I could go to a barn dance with the other kids in the neighborhood, and he said no! This upset me so much; I sneaked out of the house after dark and went to the barn dance anyway. The dance started at midnight and ended at 5:00 A.M. Well I came dragging in about 6:00 A.M. but I never got inside the house because my uncle had spread my clothes out across the front porch, nicely and neatly. Although I knew what this meant, he saw that I wasn't in bed and he was showing me that he was still the man in that house. It hurt me badly enough that my clothes were outside, but my uncle had lain a broken dinner plate on top of my clothes. I really knew what that meant. To a teenager, the message was clear.

I was also growing into a full fledged teen with my own agenda and our directions crossed occasionally. For the first time in my life I heard my uncle say, "I don't have to take care of you anymore, you're not my son."

"My world is empty without you, Jen"

I left that home and moved in with my aunt Leona (Lee), my mother's other sister. I moved in with Lee, as we called her, until I was put out of high school in my senior year.

I was at the crossroads of my life but I don't think I recognized that at the time. My only thoughts were to stay in school, play sports and maybe get a scholarship to a college where I'll have a chance to be somebody. So I immersed myself in school and sports and tried to survive long enough to graduate from high school. Well, that didn't work out either and I didn't get a scholarship or a high school diploma. Here's what happened.

After Junior High school, I chose to not attend the local neighborhood high school I wanted to change my environment and my chances to succeed. So I enrolled in a high school across town that specialized in business courses, accounting, sales, and secretarial skills. My sister and cousin Pam had attended John Hay High and Pam was still there. I'd also heard that there were about 900 girls there and 250 boys. Those were my kind of odds. I had to ride two buses to get to school and back and the school was integrated. The school was famous for being the home of the fastest typist in American high school and the worst football team on the East Side. But the school population was different. Not only were the girls prettier and more plentiful, there was an air about them that attracted me. The students seemed to dress better and act more sophisticated. The boys were "cooler" than the boys in my neighborhood and the girls seemed to all wear little lace collars on their sweaters and saddle shoes. This was going to be fun. Staying in school was not a problem, so I thought.

I played football, basketball and baseball. We didn't have a track team but that was just as well, I wasn't the fastest kid in any neighborhood. On the football team I played quarterback having learned these skills at the playground playing on gravel and asphalt. And the one thing I could really do well was to throw a football about 70 yards in the air. I was a very good baseball player and was hoping that this sport would be my ticket out of the neighborhood to a good school, and then to the pros. My weakest sport was basketball, not so much because of lack of skills, I was short for a basketball player, and almost every kid on the East Side of Cleveland could play basketball. I was only average. But ironically, basketball would be the sport that changed my life, changed my direction from being a pro baseball player or a high school graduate. Scholarships and college appeared to walk right out of the front door.

On a fateful day while practicing the day before a high school basketball tournament game, with the rain falling in sheets outside, we were playing skins against shirts working on some plays in preparation for the game the next day. I was playing right guard on defense at the time when my teammate advance toward our half of the court dribbling the ball. At the split second I saw his eyes spot the offensive center move into the lane open for a lay up and I dove toward the center of the court to intercept the ball. At the very same split second my defensive team mate playing left guard made the same move and we met in the middle of the court. As I leaped left,

Earl leaped right and we met in a violent crash resulting with both of us lying on the court. Earl got up. I didn't. I had heard a snap which sounded like bone breaking and I immediately grabbed my knee as I hit the floor hard. My scream was enough to stop the cheerleaders who were practicing on the sidelines dead in their tracks. My other team mates also rushed to where I lay to give assistance if possible. The only person who took their time getting to me was my coach, a white man who said, "Move him off the court and get back to practice." My team mates were furious and told him to get away, not to touch me.

I remember going in and out of consciousness until I reached the hospital. I remember the reaction of my girlfriend, a cheerleader was screaming at the paramedics to unzip the black bag down that I had been placed in because it looked like I was dead. They had zipped it up to keep the rain off my face when they were loading me into the ambulance. They accommodated her and it rained on my face. I didn't care I was unaware of anything but pain.

My knee cap had been broken into seven pieces.

Luckily I had been attended to by an Orthopedic Surgeon from Cleveland Clinic who performed this miracle where he pieced my knee cap back together without cutting my knee open. He used a scope and used his jig saw puzzle skills to fit the knee cap into one piece. A hip to toe cast was fitted and my healing period was supposed to be at least eight weeks in the cast and another six weeks on a cane. I was told that in a year I'd be like new. A year! To a jock a year in rehab can be fatal to your career. Well I missed the baseball season that year which was my junior year and football season was still questionable. I had missed so much school that the school system sent a Truant Officer to my home to check me out. My grades suffered and I was told that I would not graduate with my class the next year. My dreams were just *festering in the sun.*

My senior year was just a disappointment to me and I managed to make up some classes but not enough to graduate still. My baseball career was slipping away fast and my attitude was also on the slide.

In the spring of the year I had an encounter with the new Assistant Principal, a white man who called me and the other principal jocks into his office one on one to read us the Riot Act. His story was since we colored students had come to the school the school had gone down in its academics. First of all it pissed me off because I was no longer "colored" and secondly it was a lie. The academic rating had actually risen since we integrated the school seven or eight years earlier. This white man continued to pontificate about how the school jocks think we can get away with anything. He threatened to throw me and the other Negro athletes out of school if we messed up in the slightest way. I became even madder and I told him where he could take his bigoted ass. By this time we were both getting pretty loud and a student office helper heard the shouting and came into the office to break us up. He threw me out of school in my senior year, two months before graduation: and you know what? I didn't care any more.

As I watched my classmates throw their caps in the air at the graduation ceremony, I cried.

CHAPTER 22

ALTHOUGH JEN HAD BEEN DEAD for almost three years, I thought of her every day of my life and during this period I thought of her more. She was the motivating factor that kept me from becoming a criminal or maybe a drug addict. Jen had told me that I could be anything that I wanted to be and she was the only hope I had.

> *"Just because I'm a ghetto child*
> *I won't live down to your expectations.*
> *Just believe that a ghetto child*
> *Can rise in the highest celebration*
> *Know that I am a ghetto child*
> *But I can see the best in me, can you?*
> *I'm a ghetto child."*
> Lyrics by Joe

Just before I hit the bottom my cousin Julia threw me a lifeline. She was doing day work for a Jew who owned a lumber yard and she had convinced him to give me a job. My cousin Walter was also part of the deal so we went to work at the lumber yard. The first day Walter and I had to load the trucks with sheetrock to be installed in a new housing development. We were assigned to work with two white guys. One was the truck driver and the other was supposed to be a laborer the same as Walter and me. But we noticed that the white guys didn't do much work but they did a lot of smoking and taking breaks while we were told to keep working.

We worked so hard the first day that we couldn't open our hands all the way from carrying wallboard. After we loaded the trucks at the lumber yard we rode over to the housing development and unloaded the wallboard into a partially built house. The order was for 50,000 square feet of sheetrock and Walter and I hauled most of it into the houses. Again, the white guys sat in the truck smoking and listening to the radio while we worked. This went on for two more days. At the end of the third day Walter and I had had enough of the bullshit and decided to quit that job. We went in to see the boss and complained that we were doing all of the work and getting paid less money so we wanted a raise in pay. The boss refused and we quit. The owner wrote out our checks on the spot and we left. I was so mad I decided to blow the whole check on something frivolous so I bought an expensive tennis racquet which as it turns out, I used for several years, even later in college. Yes, college.

Still I had no job, no high school diploma and I seemed to be reacting to every incident of racism or discrimination passing through my life. This Negro thing is hard. There is no village in which to hide my troubles or share with the neighborhood. I was on my own. So I thought. I had forgotten about God, Jen, my family and myself.

"Lean on me when you're not strong."
Sung by Bill Withers

When I seemed to be at my lowest level there was still something in me that said to me *"Oh no. it is not over yet. I'll tell you when it's over."* Although my family would have never let me be temporarily homeless but I knew I had to do something more permanent with my life. The only person I could think of who would help me without reservation was my mother, Motherdear; whose name was Wylene. I had visited Motherdear during a few summers and I knew she had always wanted me to stay with her and go to school in Cincinnati. The only problem was that I didn't have the fare to get to Cincinnati. I called my cousin Walter and asked him if he would ride to Cincinnati with me for awhile, then he could return to Cleveland and I would stay in Cincinnati if Motherdear would have me. Walter said he would and I had to think of how to get the $10 train fare.

For some reason which I can't remember now, I asked my friend who lived above me on E. 65th Street to loan me $10.00 to buy a ticket to Cincinnati. Howard agreed to lend it to me and that $10.00 was all it took to save my life.

Our village was slowly breaking up. Life would never be the same in the village again. The village would never be the same. Today, the village is a ghost town with people still living there, but each house is its own village; not knowing or caring about whoever was living next door, this week.

CHAPTER 23

When we arrived in Cincinnati it was raining cats and dogs, so Walter and I decided to take a cab from the train station although on a dry day we would have walked the ten blocks to Motherdear's apartment. I had not told my mother that I was coming, I don't know if I was afraid of what she might say or I wanted to surprise her, make her day. When the cab pulled up to the building, I could see Motherdear sitting in her fourth floor window watching the rain. She didn't see us and when I opened her screen door and walked into the fourth floor apartment she turned around and I thought she was going to have a heart attack. I didn't think about that, she could have. My God, what a reunion. It still brings tears to my eyes remembering how I could feel her heart beat as she held me in her arms.

Of course she wanted to know what I was doing there and I told her that I was there to stay if she would let me. Then she asked if I was serious or was I going to leave her later on? She was reaching out to me as much as I was reaching out to her. We both needed each other in our lives. After we settled down and started to talk I told her about school and the first thing she said after that was that I was going to get registered to go back to school. Those were the most welcomed words I could have hoped for and there was definitely not an objection coming from me.

I was registered at Robert A. Taft High School, which was right across the street from our new apartment in the Laurel Homes. When I started school at Taft I was a year older than my classmates having already completed most of the work in the twelfth grade. I worked hard in school and received all A's and one B. I was too old at nineteen to play sports at Taft but now I was thinking about college and a renewed baseball career.

In spite of the fact that I had only been at Taft one year, the seniors voted me Prom King for which I am still grateful and I still polish the trophy presented to me at the Prom. I was feeling good about myself and as I listened to the other students at Taft talk about going to college I thought why not me, too? When I discussed the possibility with Motherdear she had no idea how that could happen. No one else in our family had ever graduated from college and she knew she couldn't help financially. I had just about agreed to get a job in the Post Office where you can make a decent living for the rest of your life, when I thought of a last resort. I had received literature from the University of Cincinnati, then a private city school, and I read about a new college in the university called University College. This college was for students who either couldn't qualify totally academically, or, wasn't sure what college to enter as a freshman. I decided to try to enroll even though it was already July. I thought of something else. The name of the high school from which I graduated was Robert A. Taft and the Taft family was still very prominent in Cincinnati. Robert A. Taft, Jr. was a U.S. Senator and I decided to get him to help me get in the university this coming semester. What did I have to lose? There was always the Post Office.

I called Senator Taft's office and made an appointment to see him. When the day came I was as nervous as can be but I knew this was another opportunity to reach my second goal that was to get in college and play baseball. I met Senator Taft and he took me to lunch at a fancy restaurant in downtown Cincinnati. We talked about my year at Taft High and I asked him directly to help me get into the University of Cincinnati. Senator Taft must have seen something in me or believed in my goal of a college education because when we got back to his office he called the Dean of the University College who happened to be in Europe on vacation. He left a message, took my phone number and I left. I was still overwhelmed by the Senator's generosity and kindness when I received a phone call from the University College to come in for an interview. My god! Is this happening to the colored, excuse me, Negro kid from the E. 65th Street village?

When I arrived at the University College Dean's Office there were two ladies sitting behind desks. I assumed they were the dean's secretaries. As I walked in the office they stood up to greet me. These white women actually stood up to greet *me*. Maybe being a Negro isn't so bad after all. It sure felt good at that moment. The Dean was a pleasant man who after a long talk registered me for the University College. I was actually a college student. This was Cool.

Chapter 24

BACK IN 1969 I WROTE AN ARTICLE for a local Newspaper by the title, "Police, the Smallest Minority". I wrote it to show that cops seem to do the same things and shield each other from outside criticism because they are all they have. All of their friends are cops and just like a minority group they are the only ones defending their actions or giving them any respect. Everyone else seems to look at them as a necessary evil and in some cases the enemy. Remember Rudy and Three Finger Johnson I talked about earlier in this book? Well they were Negro cops assigned to patrol our Negro neighborhood. They would show up on the block and everyone seemed to freeze in place. It was like one of those horror movies where time stood still. All activities came to a halt even the kids stopped to watch them. The cops seemed to enjoy this form of intimidation and control over their own people. I guess it was the power that corrupted them. Rudy's reputation was so great that all he had to do was get out of his parked car, number 528, and bang his night stick on a metal utility pole and immediately the neighborhood changed its demeanor. Were they there to protect and serve? Of course not, they were there to intimidate us and make themselves feel good. As far as we were concerned they were a clear and present danger to us and everybody else in the neighborhood. That's sad, but true.

In the late fifties the principal weapon of the policeman, besides the gun, was a nightstick which was used frequently as their enforcement tool. Everybody knew that if you made a cop angry or if they were in a bad mood you would get hit with the stick. I found that out personally the very night before I was to report for college. I had come home from Cincinnati to see the family and say goodbye to my girlfriend whom I had left in Cleveland when I moved to Cincinnati the year before. So when I was returning from her house out in the near suburb making my way home, feeling both sad from leaving her and happy for what was ahead, I had stayed so long that I missed the last bus from her neighborhood. So the only thing to do was to walk to the end of the line and wait until the buses started running again in a few hours.

My girl's neighborhood was just inside the white community and it was about 2 AM and as I was walking toward the bus line I noticed ahead of me a parked police car. I also noticed that there were two figures, cops I presumed, standing by the car. This made me as nervous as if I had run into a street gang that I wasn't friendly with. As I approached the two police officers I saw that they were white and had nightsticks in their hands. My first reaction was Oh shit! What now? I can't run that's an invitation to be shot. I can't cross the street that would really escalate the situation, so I just gritted my teeth and walked straight ahead. My stomach felt like someone was dancing the Macarena in there and when the cops split up, one on each side of the sidewalk, I knew I was going to get hurt. The only thing for me to do was to walk right between them and keep on going. Good plan huh? As I got even with the cops my heart was beating so loudly I know they heard it because I think they tried to stop the noise with their sticks. One cop hit me in the solar plexus and the other hit me just below the chest. I doubled over and grunted in pain. I think I was probably more stunned than hurt because of the adrenalin pulsing through my veins. When I straightened up one of the cops shouted "What the hell are you doing in this neighborhood this time of night?" When I was able to speak I said that I was walking to the end of the bus line to catch a bus home. The other cop repeated the question saying "Well what the hell are you doing in this neighborhood?" I told them the story that my girl lived near there and I was going away to college the next day and I was saying goodbye to her. Well one of them said he didn't believe that I was going to college and that I had better get the f--- out of this neighborhood all the while poking me with his nightstick. I said "yes sir" and continued my walk down the street only with a more bent over posture now. I guess I can consider myself lucky that the only weapon they had to intimidate me with was a night stick. Just think if they had stun guns or Tazers to try out on me at 2AM in the morning. No one would have known or come to my rescue after all I was walking through a white neighborhood telling what they undoubtedly thought was a bullshit story like going to college the next day.

The point is two things: (1) Those cops felt powerful enough and empowered enough to hit me, a teenager, a Negro teenager with their night sticks for no reason at all, and (2) they would have used whatever new device they would have been issued to subdue a potential perpetrator just for amusement. *Their amusement.*

I believe because of their insecurities for being the smallest minority they overcompensate with force and intimidation. We've issued them all of these weapons and the authority to use them indiscriminately. This supposedly makes them feel more powerful, with more self-esteem, and in control. Just like other minorities they feel that nobody likes them except other cops, and that everybody is out to get them so they must be aggressive. If not for self protection, why would it take ten cops to subdue one person, or five cops to beat a person or tazer a person unnecessarily just to quiet them down or get them under control? Or worse, shoot and kill a retarded child holding a knife in his own home.

Believe me, I'm not saying disarm the policeman just train them better with the attitude that these dangerous new high tech weapons should only be used for the extreme cases when police control is really threatened. A cop must be held accountable for the misuse of dangerous weapons such as tazers the same as with guns. Punishment should also be meted out to rid the force of those who can not control themselves under stressful situations. Heaven forbid if a hand held nuclear powered weapon is developed for crowd control one day. Half our neighborhoods would be blinded or irradiated for a thousand years.

CHAPTER 25

IT ONLY TAKES ONE AHH SHIT to wipe out Two Attaboys. Well someone hollered Ahh Shit when I wasn't looking because the baseball thing didn't work out. Oh I went out for the college team alright. I think I looked very good in fielding and hitting. I did notice that in the locker room there was only one white boy who would sit with me and talk to me. The other white kids had nothing to say during any practice. I was the only Negro trying out for the team and I knew I could play ball at this level, I had been scouted and invited to play in a summer professional rookie league when I was fifteen, and my knee injury was healed. But after one of the practice session the locker room was awful quiet when my friend and I came in. On the bulletin board was the list of the kids who had made the team. With the same enthusiasm that the other kids had shown, I looked at the list for my name. It wasn't there. Maybe it was a mistake, I can play ball. I'm going to be a major leaguer one day. As happy as I felt when I became a college student, I was just as hurt when the whole locker room was watching me in dead silence. I didn't want those guys to see me cry so I gathered up my stuff out of the locker and left the building. I cried all the way to the Athletic Director's office where I confronted the A.D. about not making the team. Reluctantly I was told that the university schedule for the coming two seasons was not ready for a Negro player. That if I had patience maybe in a few years I could try out again. The schedule had some southern schools on it that wouldn't play against a Negro player and it would take a couple years for the university to reschedule different schools. I brought up the fact that Oscar Robertson had played basketball in the south for the university, why not me? The AD explained that southern schools allow play against basketball teams with Negroes but not yet baseball. Come back in a few years. *"Come back in a few years?"* I don't have a few years my dream is being deferred. Now.

> *"I'm so hurt to think that you lied to me*
> *I'm hurt way down deep inside of me."*

Words and music: J. Crane/A. James

I was so bitter over this I decided not to just get mad and stomp away, I was going to dedicate my life fighting bigotry and discrimination wherever it exists. That was not just an empty promise or a cliche; I actually did it and am still doing it in my own way. For the next three years our civil right organization at school tried to make it as uncomfortable as we could for the university when discrimination and racism was encountered or anticipated. We solicited the help from the university's greatest hero, Oscar Robertson who volunteered to help us. We were moving to another level, being Negro was out, we were Black and proud. Black Power!

> *"Say it Loud, I'm Black and I'm proud."*
> Sung by James Brown

For a long time I hated baseball. I couldn't even watch a baseball game on television for years afterwards.

It was two years later that the University had its first Black baseball player; my fraternity brother Darrell.

Ten years later I had graduated, married, moved my children and wife from Cincinnati to Fort Wayne, Indiana and then to Kalamazoo, Michigan. While working as a young executive at a meat packing plant I played softball with the company team. One evening after work while playing in a league game, I made a couple of great fielding plays to retire the batters. After the game a couple of white guys came over to me and asked if they could talk to me. They had watched me play, they said, a couple of weeks and wanted to know if I would play with their team sponsored by Burger King. They were playing in a higher league and playing games regionally. They talked about playing in tournaments and winning championships and honors. My mind starting wondering back to the days when I wanted to be a major league player and it made my heart pump so fast I thought it was going to jump out of my chest. I said yes.

When I went to the first practice, I could see that I was the only Black player on the squad and the white guys treated me with open arms. I made the team and was to play third base in the next game.

I really felt like a bona fide ball player when I put on that great looking uniform and cap from Burger King. The first game was going to be my coming out game where I was going to show the world that all of that time learning to "hook slide" and fielding "short hops" and talking to the Athletic Director about playing ball in college was to be the basis for a new career in sports that I could tell my children about proudly.

The crowd was good, the weather was perfect, my family was there and all eyes, I thought, were on me at third base. I was nervous but I knew I could play this game and I would let that assurance and confidence get me through. The game progressed through the first inning without me having to field a ball. But this wasn't going to last either.

The second inning started with a hit to left center field and the runner advanced to second base. This drew me back closer to third base in case of a steal attempt or a hit that would advance the runner to third. The next hitter pulled a grounder down the third base line and I knew in my head that I had a clean catch all the way. I remembered the hundreds of times I had made this play and fielded the ball as cleanly and sharply as any major leaguer on TV. All I had to do now was throw the runner out at first base as the runner on second held his position on the base. I wound up knowing that hardly anyone could outrace my bullet-like throw to first base and I let the ball fly on its maiden flight from my hand. Our pitcher knew from practice that when I fielded a ball at third, he had better move back or duck so that I wouldn't hit him with the ball. He moved and

I threw the ball with my usual power but the ball went directly in front of me into the dirt. The crowd gasped and my teammates were shocked into silence. I didn't know what had happened, except now my shoulder hurt so bad I couldn't raise it any more. As I doubled over I let out a grunt which signaled my teammates and everyone there that something had gone horribly wrong.

I had thrown my arm out. Maybe for good. My serious softball career was over. It didn't take a tearful talk with the Manager to know that. I gathered my things and my family and left the ball diamond. The Manager came to our house and picked up the uniform a day or so later.

Where is Jen, Billy and the village now?

CHAPTER 26

I DON'T THINK WE WILL EVER have true equality in America. There will never be a day when *"little black boys and black girls will be able to join hands with little white boys and white girls as sisters and brothers."* (Dr. Martin Luther King) There will be instances when it looks like equality and feels like equality, but every time an incident occurs where a Black child is denied an opportunity, or membership, or a job, or misjudged by the legal system, or expelled from school discriminatorily, or when a Black person is denied a promotion from the back rooms of corporate American woodsheds, or when White Americans continue to hide behind patriotism rather than face the truth, or wrap themselves in the American flag as if it only belongs to them, or still treat Blacks as if we were visitors in America not Americans, or when a new generation of red necks are born, or a group of Neo-Nazis form, or when a White child hears their parent call a Black person a "nigger" then we know that nothing has really changed except our villages were disbanded and we were dispersed around the land. Urban Renewal Programs also helped with the dispersements.

Overt racism is cyclical. We are seeing an upsurge in overt racism reminiscent of the fifties and early sixties. It was pretty common in the fifties and sixties to pick up a newspaper and read about a Black person being mutilated or physical confrontations between the races, or schools being segregated as well as communities. Well when you read a newspaper in 2012 you can read about the same kinds of stories as you did then. Racism is on the rise in America and White people seem to be getting more comfortable with it all the time. After 50 years I can still picture bare-chested White bigots screaming profanities at Black people at peaceful demonstrations. I see the American justice system meting out punishment on an unequal basis; one that will do anything to get O.J. Simpson behind bars. I still read about Central High School in Little Rock, Arkansas where after deploying the U.S. Army in order to integrate the school in 1957, it is still as segregated as it was fifty-five years ago. Only now on the inside.

During the last forty years "civil rights" has stood in the corner of our homes and schools like the little black statues of jockeys holding a lamp. Nobody talked about it (civil rights) or tried to keep it alive we felt comfortable that it was there. Also during that time new generations were born who had never experienced the pain and suffering of the civil rights movement, didn't understand what the black jockey statue meant. They just threw their hats on it and kept on going. Now they are experiencing the same issues, questions and feelings that we experienced in the sixties. The difference is that nobody is answering those questions today. Maybe that is why Rev. Al Sharpton declared the Jena 6 incident the rebirth of the Civil Rights Movement. Just like the Jena 6 crisis, the incident at the Model Secondary School for the Deaf on October 4, 2007, teenagers, students in school, was crude and indicative of uninformed young people who are ignorant of the Civil Rights Movement and all it stood for. Six white, and get this, one Black student detained a Black student and drew "KKK and swastikas" on his body. What were they thinking, was this a joke? They obviously have no idea what it took in blood and lives to make it possible for white and black students to go to school together. It traumatized the black student who reported the incident to school officials, who did understand the significance of this incident and called the Police. We are tired of the insults, and the meaningless apologies. Somebody needs to wake the Movement up and wake us up. We can't afford another generation to be raised uninformed and ignorant about why equality is worth fighting for and dying for. *When we were colored we understood this.*

CHAPTER 27

THE WORDS THAT RESONATED from the mouth of the great Dr. Martin Luther King, Jr. echoed off every mountain and building in the free world that day in 1963. At no time were we more hopeful than when Dr. King said, *"Free at last, free at last, Thank God almighty I'm free at last."* These words will forever occupy a position next to other recognizable phrases such as *"Four score and seven years ago"* and *"Give me liberty or give me death"*. But unlike the historical confrontations prompting those words of Abraham Lincoln and Patrick Henry, our war against racism and discrimination still rages. Dr. King's words seem to have motivated the enemy more than our fellow citizenry. White business, corporate America, discriminate at alarming rates every day with no concern about consequences. There is not a second thought given to not hiring African Americans, or promoting them to more responsible positions. None at all. Corporate America knows that first of all, the African American is not going to do anything about it. Secondly, to whom are they going to complain? Blacks are intimidated and will not risk losing their jobs. There will be no help coming. It's corporate America who is proclaiming in those corporate woodsheds, *"Free at last, free at last . . ."*

Just recently, I wrote a book called "What Your Black Friends Don't Tell You" which expressed my sentiments and feelings about racism. With race hatred and intimidation on the rise in America, and opposition to racism still not popular with politicians or their constituency, ordinary citizens need to step up and re-awaken the giant that is civility and justice that usually characterizes America. "What Your Black Friends Don't Tell You" will stir up the sleeping masses to again demand and insure racial equality and justice before it is too late, and the American norm takes on the appearance of the black and white days of the 1940s and 1950s where African Americans and Hispanics will have to take a deep breath before walking into what would normally be a friendly assembly of white Americans.

Benign neglect has caused Americans to become so drowsy you would think that drugs are an every day staple on the American family breakfast table.

"What Your Black Friends Don't Tell You" will surprise some, anger some, rekindle the human spirit in some, re-establish partnerships of the sixties and seventies, and make some laugh, but its main point is to get you to talk to your Black friends at work, politicians in your cities and your neighbors to dispel the myth that there is no race problem in America anymore. What you are seeing today is the shaking off of the *"chains of intimidation"* of Black people who are now speaking out. You are about to witness the rebirth of the Civil Rights Movement all over again.

I believe the book will appeal to a wide audience because there is something in the book that can make each reader shake their head in agreement, or, say "yeah that's right". What the book then demands is that each reader share their thoughts and feelings with another. Start a snowball of discussions in church, the grocery store, at work. Once we learn to speak out about racism, only then will racism become a whisper in the back room of a racist's mind.

The book is one man's opinion about racism in America and how it is *still* very prevalent and frightening. But hopefully the book will encourage others to say what is on their minds, and talk about the discrimination and racist acts that are happening to them *still* today. There is not only an economic crisis going on but a racial crisis also. And, America has always been able to multitask to solve everyone else's problems, why not do it for ourselves? We can start by putting the subject back on the Congressional Agenda in Washington. We have let white America off the hook in the last twenty years by not raising the issue of racism. It has been as if we were all too scared to breach the subject. It seems that if Rev. Sharpton didn't bring up an issue in New York mainly with the NYPD, there wouldn't be any discussion.

It is my hope that this book raises the temperature to the point of discomfort so that someone in Washington and South Carolina and Illinois and Oregon and all the other forty-six states will get warm enough to deal with the "Continental Warming" right here in America. America is not a village, the village is dead.

"What Your Black Friends Don't Tell You" also has a lighter side (pun intended). The book attempts to introduce the subject of cultural differences in a way that is not only historic, but humorous. When important decisions are made today about cultural issues such as language, fashion, entertainment and lifestyle, white America has to make it imperative to include Black America in the mix. I know how hard that is because white America has to learn to think like Black Americans. This probably sounds crazy but I tried to learn to speak Spanish and couldn't. I was told that I need to think like a Hispanic to really learn to speak the language. "What Your Black Friends Don't Tell You" has given white America a headstart by talking about how much easier it would be just to include our cultural contributions in everyday life.

My book was one of the books featured at the Los Angeles Times Festival of Books in 2012, held at the University of Southern California sponsored by my publisher, AuthorHouse and can be purchased at your favorite local book seller.

CHAPTER 28

THERE HASN'T BEEN ANY PRESSURE by the Federal Government since the seventies about hiring discrimination. All of the advocacy agencies are dead or ineffective. Where is the NAACP and the Urban League? Off throwing conventions and dances for the socialization of their boards and white friends in corporate America. What happened to the Civil Rights Commission? Has it suffered from benign neglect along with the rest of us? They were supposed to be manning the Watch Tower all of these years since the Movement, but the tower is empty. There is no sentry on duty there. Is there no war left to be fought against racism and discrimination? Let me remind you of something else Mr. Patrick Henry said in his speech to the second Virginia Convention in 1775:

> *"It is in vain, sir, to extenuate the matter. Gentlemen may cry, Peace, Peace but there is no peace. The war is actually begun! The next gale that sweeps from the north will bring to our ears the clash of resounding arms! Our brethren are already in the field! Why stand we here idle? What is it that gentlemen wish? What would they have? Is life so dear, or peace so sweet, as to be purchased at the price of chains and slavery? Forbid it, Almighty God! I know not what course others may take; but as for me, give me liberty or give me death!"*

It may be a good idea for the NAACP and the Urban League to open every meeting of the Boards of Directors with this quotation just to remind them that a war is still raging all around them and colored people are still suffering at the hands of racists and bigots in our schools, factories, and neighborhoods. Maybe they can "act" like a civil rights organization again even if this is not their agenda for the new century. Most colored people think that they still are our sentries manning those watch towers in urban America.

The NAACP and the Urban League used to be a part of the village when I was colored. They were within reach of the villagers. Now they occupy high rent district locations, not so easy to reach. As my wife was reading the October 2012 NAACP letter talking about the 41 states that are trying to make it impossible for African Americans and Hispanics to vote, she asked me a very important question, "Does everyone get this letter, because everyone ought to read this.?" We both wondered if the people in the villages get the same message and information as the financial supporters. I hope this information gets to the village people because it is so important they know who the enemies are and who is still trying to hold them down.

Maybe I'm wrong. Maybe since I don't live in the village anymore I might be out of touch. Well if I'm out of touch so are millions of Black people which still suggests that our leadership organizations need to better commercialize their programs so that we'll know where to go when we need help. I might not be a villager anymore but I am still African American and I still need to know that someone has my back.

I still remember Roy Wilkerson and Whitney Young when I was colored; I wonder if this generation knows who the leadership of the NAACP and the Urban League is today.

I am seventy-two years old. Soon to be seventy-three. A year ago I talked to a gentleman through email who remembers me from 1957 when he and I worked for a local hospital in Cleveland, Ohio. As a matter of fact, he followed me in a job progression from dishwasher to Pots and Pans Washer. We made ninety cents an hour, and on Friday night we thought we were "Phat", Pretty Hot and Tempting.

It is now 2012 and I probably don't have too many long hot summer days left. Not many happy holiday seasons or arguments about who will win the Super Bowl. I have been blessed all of my life having had the opportunity to father two sons, whom I don't always understand, but I love. I've lived in places children of ten only dream of as distant, far away lands. I've seen things that most of my people have never even heard of let alone seen. I have no regrets, only pain. Pain because I know that all of the touching of ancient objects, standing on holy grounds, seeing the most beautiful sights God has created, riding in hot air balloons, seeing things that are surely wonders of the world will soon be gone with the memory of me. I have watched Black men knock holes in huge shells and remove the living creatures inside, and I have walked through an underpass in London with the words, "God Is Dead" signed Nietzsche, and another sign that read, Nietzsche is dead", signed God scrawled on the walls. I have given dimes to dozens of small children in a jungle village in Mexico who were begging for pennies and attention. There is pain because at my age I may never see such wonderful things again. This is not a swan song, I am not anticipating leaving this earth or this body, I just know that the "ultama test" as Richard Pryor stated, can come at any time now and these life experiences will pass from wonderments to memories to puffs of necrological nebulosity.

I know that each and every one of you, who are reading this today can stop, put your heads back and visualize similar wonderful things in your life. Things that you hang on to through your memories, pictures or conversations with those who share them with you. But now think, think of all those things and then make a list of those memories that have made a significant difference in your life or the life of others. Think of the things that may impact the world or even the environment you live in. The list is probably pretty small if not non-existent. This is why I long to be a part of something significant at my age, make the big score, witness an act that will change lives in the world or my environment while I am still alive. I can say that having worked in the original Civil Rights Movement of the sixties I have experienced just that kind of change. Living through school integration or the opening up of job opportunities that had been closed to Blacks, or Black people moving to neighborhoods previously guarded and protected, even by law, for whites only. I have lived through that kind of change and am proud to have been a part of the change as an agent. Pain, because I want to be a part of that kind of change again, one more time. So I look for another opportunity to "become".

I have become an author. I write books, books about things I know; Civil Rights. I believe that maybe some of what I am saying will reach an ear that will let my words linger there long enough to be referred to later on when a decision needs to be made about one's path in life. I write about things I know, things about my life experiences, about what I feel about the way my life has been impacted by others such as racists and intimidators and just plain people who have apparent power over my life. My "one more time" will be in the books I write and the reaction from those who read them. I found my new way to "become" through my writings. I use to march, carry signs, sing about freedom, go to rallies, talk to teenagers on the streets, lecture to college age youngsters about Black History, now, I write.

You see, at seventy-two years old, I still want to make a difference. I still want to be a part of something significant. Remember the saying, "Old soldiers never die, they just fade away"? Well I don't want to just fade away; I'd like to be remembered as being a part of something meaningful, something good. To be someone who in his old age has finally thrown off the yoke of intimidation and stood up to racism and injustice.

Wouldn't all you old folks like me want to see a show of unity from our people that have the power to change the world? Wouldn't we like to be a part of that kind of a movement? That's what I'm talking about when I speak of doing something significant, making a difference. How would it be to be a part of the movement to re-elect a man of color to the Presidency of the United States? Not just vote for the winning person, be he or she Democrat or Republican, but actually have your vote count in a significant discernible way; just one more time before we die. That would be the height of "self-determination" the over used phrase that is still hanging out in front of African Americans like the proverbial carrot on a stick. Then why wouldn't we try? I'll tell you why.

Chapter 29

I CANNOT LEAVE THIS DISCUSSION just by blaming the breakup of the village on geography and racism, although they have to bear their share of the blame.

Ever since I can remember African Americans have been mistrustful of other African Americans. Whether fussin' about who took the last piece of sweet potato pie or who is the head of the Civil Rights Movement, or whether President Obama is doing a good job, we don't trust each other. Envy, jealousy, lust, greed, sloth, pride and gluttony, the cardinal sins of early Christianity are alive and well and living amongst us. Amongst our "so called" leadership, of whom many are preachers, and amongst our people "en masse" who cannot seem to communicate for the common good at any time. Not even during the tailor made opportunity with the "Jena Six"; or the death of Trayvon Martin, which should have rung out as the rebirth of the "Civil Rights Movement" in America. Now we have a serious African American running for re-election as President of the United States of America, and we are still taking sides with the other white candidates just to spite someone, or, protect our precious TV time, or feeble reputations. We have even gone so far as to say in public, "We are still waiting for the first Black President". Like many African Americans, I too am a little disappointed in the results of President Obama's first four years. But, I know that he inherited the biggest mess since the Depression and its taking longer to solve thanks to the non-cooperation of the Republican Party.

If you are familiar with political science you will understand that the Presidency is hopefully a two term job and being a first term President you will have to compromise on some things that your constituency thinks is the most important business he should undertake. With the Republicans trying to guarantee he will not succeed and with the help of the Tea Party and the 1018 government and racist hate groups in the United States he is lucky to have accomplished as much as he did.

It does not bother me that President Obama is not perceived as a "Black President" because I understand what some of the pressures are that he is living through and still trying to keep America afloat. And I understand that he is the American President representing 100 percent of Americans, not just the 47% the white presidential candidate has written off. I believe that a second term President Obama will be a different person, not worrying about re-election. The second term he will be trying to make a place in history, and that effort will be vastly different that his first term.

It is my feeling that we should have worked toward getting the President re-elected and stop worrying that he doesn't wear a dashiki or an Afro haircut just to look or be Black. He was Black four years ago when we were so excited to have the chance to vote for a Black man to the highest office in the world, he is still Black, and may have been even Blacker if we had helped him get re-elected to a second term.

If we just wanted a President who acted Black or took a harder stand against racism at the possible peril of not getting anything done, then we should not have re-elected President Obama. But, if we want a President, who is Black, to work towards making America a wonderful, safe place to live and raise children, then we needed to vote him back into office. At least we knew there was a chance that he would address issues that affect African Americans, but we also know what we will get by losing him; more benign neglect from a white President.

Wake up Black People! I never even conceived an African American President in my lifetime, or my children's. The history books will be written differently in the future and his face will be as prominent as Abraham Lincoln or JFK. I believe him to be a President that we can tell our grandchildren and great—grandchildren about. Proudly!

I remember when we were all "colored" and living in small villages across America, yet we were all the same because it was clear what we wanted and needed. We need those villages back again so we can stop the nonsense that seems to come with being African American. It really doesn't matter what we call ourselves does it? When we were Afro-Americans, Negro or Black racism was still prevalent and holding us down.

Just once we ought to be strong enough to put our "penny anny" differences aside and show some solidarity.

I say to our leadership, the NAACP, the Urban League, the Congressional Black Caucus, just once before you old men and old women die wouldn't you like to do something significant, make a difference? You know deep down in your hearts that when the chips are down, African Americans cannot expect any reliable help from anyone but us.

"Behold, how good and how pleasant it is for Brothers to dwell together in unity." Psalms 133:1NAS

There is a new wave on the not-so-distant horizon and it is moving this way rapidly. The next few generations of civil rights leaders after us old men and women may not be African Americans at all. We are nearing our last few chances to make a stand; and maybe push back on that wave coming our way.

The Southern Poverty Law Center (SPLC) has stated that there were 1,018 hate and antigovernment groups in America in 2011. What a great base for the racists and haters to use to build a different America. An America that doesn't include the "affected classes or people of color" (colored people) in the mix.

Chapter 30

BILLY DIED LAST MONTH and I still haven't gotten over his death, even though we saw each other or talked infrequently as adults. He taught me everything I knew as a young man, but he couldn't stop the pain I lived through as an adult being African American. When I was ten years old, in the fifth grade I used to dream about being sixty years old, in the year 2000. Maybe because of the suffering over the years between being colored and being African American was the reason in the year 2000, I dreamed of again being ten years old. Being colored; not having to know about Emmitt Till, Travon Martin, still fighting for the right to vote in an election in America and others. Remembering watching the white children in Shaker Heights look at me through their windows and me wondering if they wanted to play with me or chase me out of their village.

I know we'll never have the villages back again as they were before, but the mentality of the village can live on in us forever and take us to the "highest celebration".

In many ways, I miss the village.

www.ingramcontent.com/pod-product-compliance
Lightning Source LLC
Chambersburg PA
CBHW030349290526
45785CB00004B/1662